Rollercoaster
COLIN

Portrait of Colin Nightingale

by Christine Stannard

Rollercoaster
COLIN

A Memoir

by

COLIN NIGHTINGALE

The Choir Press

Copyright © 2024 Colin Nightingale

All rights reserved. No part of this publication may be reproduced or transmitted in any form or by any means, electronic or mechanical including photocopying, recording or any information storage or retrieval system, without prior permission in writing from the publishers.

The right of Colin Nightingale to be identified as the author of this work has been asserted by him in accordance with the Copyright, Designs and Patents Act 1988

Some names in the book have been changed to protect their privacy.

First published in the United Kingdom in 2024 by
The Choir Press

ISBN 978-1-78963-427-3

Dedication

To all those who triumph over adversity

Acknowledgements

I started writing this book at the grand young age of eighty-three. As you read it, you will notice I have been on a rollercoaster ride through life. However, the trials, tribulations and the events I have written about in this book are correct as far as my eighty-three-year-old brain can remember. Any errors are completely unintentional.

I would like to thank a number of people who have helped me in writing this book:

My good friends Sandra and David McCulloch

Sandra – for her initial encouragement to write my book and her support throughout

David – for his computer and photography skills

Ajaz Qureshi – for his advice

Maryam Hussein – for her computer skills

Christine Stannard – for her portrait of Colin

My wife, Gillian – for the photography of Bird Haven, for helping me to fill in the gaps that I had forgotten, for her constant encouragement and diligent work in compiling the contents of the book

Also, many of our friends, too numerous to mention by name, for their support throughout the process

Contents

Acknowledgements		vi
Foreword		viii
Chapter One	Master Colin Early Years (Birth–12 years)	1
Chapter Two	Colin – Teenage Years (13–19 years)	9
Chapter Three	Colin – Mr Casino Twenties (21–32 years)	22
Chapter Four	Colin – Mr Belle Vue Thirties (33–42 years)	41
Chapter Five	Colin – Mr Try Anything Forties (43–50 years)	57
Chapter Six	Colin – Mr C&G Fifties (50–60 years)	71
Chapter Seven	Colin – Mr Various & Councillor Colin Sixties (60–72 years)	76
Chapter Eight	Colin – Mr Bird Haven Seventies (72–81 years)	89
Chapter Nine	Colin – Mr Eighties Eighties (82–the present)	117
Chapter Ten	Mr Colin Conclusions	121

Foreword

The author takes us through his life experiences. He starts by detailing his memories of the Second World War and tells of his school life and then his time in the forces.

He worked in many casinos in the north of England meeting many singers and groups popular at that time, and later at Belle Vue Zoo and Amusement Park in Manchester.

He tells us about serving as a local councillor, owning a shop and building a nature trail. Explaining about the ups and downs of his life, his determination to be the best and make the most of each situation.

Rollercoaster
COLIN

COLIN OLIVER NIGHTINGALE

BORN 9th NOVEMBER 1938

HARMONDSWORTH, STAINES, MIDDLESEX

CHAPTER ONE

Master Colin Early Years (Birth–12 years)

∽

I was born on the 9th of November 1938 at 17.20 on Wednesday evening. I did not get any tea, which upset me and I cried all night. I was born to Daisy and James Nightingale. I was the youngest of three children; I had a brother, Alan, who was five years older, and a sister, Jean, who was two years older. Being born in 1938, I do not remember much first-hand, but I was told later that the Second World War started in September 1939.

My first recollections are of my first days at Harmondsworth Infants' School. We were told that if an air-raid alarm sounded, we were to get down on our knees and block our ears with our hands. The air-raid alarm was a loud high-pitched noise which resonated throughout the area. Everyone would hear it and it could not be missed.

At home we had a box ottoman which was put up against the wall when the alarm sounded. The three children would hide between the wall and the extended arm of the ottoman for safety. This would give us some protection, should the house be hit from a falling bomb.

I remember lying in bed one night; it was dark and quiet. Suddenly a large pane of glass from a window blew inwards. The pane did not break, but the curtains moved inwards with the window pane forced against it. It landed across my bed; it was very frightening. Mum came in, lifted me out of bed and carried me downstairs to relative safety. I was then comforted by Mum and Dad.

Shortly after that we were given an Anderson shelter. This type of shelter was like a metal shed, which was partially dug into the back garden. It was then covered with grass or anything else from the garden, to disguise it from the enemy. We would use the shelter to sleep in if the alarm sounded. The bed frame base was put across the entrance with a mattress in front of that; this was to protect us from falling shrapnel and other debris from the bombs. We would then wait for the all-clear alarm before we went back to the house. We also had gas masks – mine was a Mickey Mouse one – to protect us from gas. We took these gas masks with us to school and everywhere we went. We even took them with us to the shelters, whether at home or at school.

I never knew what war was. I remember that Mum always listened to the radio; the name Churchill was mentioned a lot. There were posters on the walls of a man wearing a peak cap. The words read, YOUR COUNTRY NEEDS YOU!!! I was probably about five years old when the word war was mentioned more often. I remember I was always looking up to the sky, fascinated by groups of planes flying overhead. There would be groups of planes, sometimes small and sometimes large, up to a dozen. They seemed to me to fill the sky. At the time I did not know what these planes were, but later I was told that they were our pilots going on sorties. When war was over, there were street parties everywhere. The streets were lined with flags, and tables were laid with food and drink in the streets. We were allowed to go. Everybody was in the streets; there was an air of excitement and relaxed celebration, the like of which we had not experienced before.

DAD

I don't know much about my dad. His name was James Henry Hearne Nightingale. He died when I was five years old and he had a history of bad health, due to heavy smoking. I was told he was known as a jack-the-lad type and he had a short fuse. He once picked a fight with my school headmaster. He went to hit him, but the headmaster moved out of the way and Dad punched a metal post instead, which broke his hand. He did not like people who held positions of authority; he would act first without thinking of the consequences.

Another time, he bundled a Jehovah's Witness out of the doorway, after Mum had let him in. He hated them because of what they stood for, and he was not a religious man.

On the good side, he cared for me and often carried me home when we went out. Once, I was looking over his shoulder as my dad carried me. I noticed a man following us. "Hello, man," I shouted.

After our dad died, Alan had to become head of the house. He was five years older than me and would have been about ten years old. He did his best to fill Dad's shoes and would do anything for anyone.

MUM

Mum was born Daisy Roache and was brought up in a hard Victorian world, with strict disciplinarian values. She worked in service before she married James, with a well-to-do family in Holland Park, London. She would work for many hours doing household chores, from cleaning to washing, polishing floors to laying fires. She had board, food and a wage. Daisy married James and became Daisy Nightingale. They moved to a house called Carlton Villa, in Hatch Lane, Harmondsworth. The house was semi-detached with a garden at the back. There were two bedrooms upstairs, one for Daisy and James and one other. Downstairs was the parlour with a range and a sitting room. As time went by, Alan was born, then Jean and lastly myself – Colin. Mum looked after us all as best she could. We did not have much money, so Mum would stay up at night knitting socks and gloves which she could then sell for extra money.

In the house, the parlour was the main room where we had our meals and spent most of our time. It had a range with a metal platform for the kettle. Underneath was the fire to heat the kettle, and the fire was held in by a metal grid. We would toast the bread held by a long fork against the grid, and if we were lucky we would get jam on the toast. We usually had plenty of jam because in the garden we had a number of fruit trees, which kept us well stocked with apples, pears and cherries. The fire was kept alight and was the only heating for a very cold house. I remember the toilet was often frozen. We would heat the kettle and use the water to melt the ice. Another pleasure was the toilet paper, which was very hard. It was either old newspapers or, if we had the money, we would have IZAL toilet paper, which was even worse.

The food we had was basic. Of course, during the war, we were on rations like every family. If we had any meat, it would be the cheapest of cuts, which would be cooked for a very long time to soften the gristle. Most of us children detested this. We had a meal at lunchtime. If we did not eat it all, it would be served again at teatime. We would be punished severely if we still refused to eat it.

Another treat (!) we had at this time was cod liver oil. I hated it; it made me feel sick. I was punished repeatedly because I would not take it. Eventually, Mum decided to give me some malt. This was sweeter and I could stomach that. I was given the cod liver oil followed straightaway by the malt. This worked as I only tasted the malt, which was not too bad.

At Christmas, things were a bit better for us. We kept chickens in the back garden so Christmas lunch consisted of chicken and potatoes, also grown in the garden. One of our neighbours killed the chicken for us. He cut its head off. I was curious to see what he was doing. The chicken suddenly jumped up on its feet and was running round the garden minus its head! I was so frightened that I ran down the path towards the house. I was screaming because the chicken was following me. Mum came out to see what the commotion was. I ran into her. She told me to look back. I saw the chicken was now in a heap, dead on the garden path.

Throughout the war years, the house was often damaged from the air raids, with parts of the house crumbling and falling apart. I can remember coming home from school to see the window frames and doors hanging from their mountings.

Mum didn't like many people; she looked down on them. She did have a few friends, mainly those with money and property, though they never gave any help or left anything in their wills when they died.

Our school was just outside the village. Beside the school there was a large grassed play area, which consisted of swings, a seesaw, a sandpit and a putting green. We were allowed to play there, but not to go down the alley to the village. We would get in serious trouble if Mum found out we had set foot in the village. Mum thought it was low class, but we did go and she never knew. It was a quaint village, with a village store called Berries and a public house called the Three Bells, which had a small room to the side where you could get fruit juice with ice cream for 2d, a bargain in those days. And there was a large church with a small graveyard and a village hall used for public gatherings. As time went on, the war took its toll on all of these buildings. On one visit to the village we saw Berries' roof was completely missing. The wood from the roof was hanging down and some was piled up on the pavement outside. You could clearly see the damaged rafters, some still in place and others leaning against the shop wall. Other buildings were damaged as a result of an air raid.

Shortly after the war, we moved to Hayes, Middlesex. We lived on the outskirts of the town with just a few shops. We settled in at 81 Crowland Avenue near Cranford Woods, where we were able to play. This move changed my life.

In Cranford Woods there was a river, a lake and a newt pond. There was a wooden walk-way which led to the river, surrounded by bulrushes. There was also a mansion house in the middle of the woods. Years later, I watched an episode of the sixties TV series *The Persuaders*. I was surprised to see that it had been filmed there. I never thought I would see a place that I knew on the TV. Tony Curtis and Roger Moore played the star roles.

On the way to the woods we saw army trucks full of men. Local children ran along behind them. We were told the men were prisoners of war and they were being put to work, to build pre-fabricated houses in the Carfax Road area.

I attended Cranford Park School. Mum took me every day because we didn't have any friends in the new area. I was bullied in school; I did not know what a swear word was or how a dirty joke worked. The local bully always seemed to find me. One day he was sitting on a fence calling me names. I lost my temper and knocked him down. That was not a good idea. He got me back and beat me up, so I learnt to keep out of his way. I was about nine years old at the time and scared for my life. I didn't tell anybody about my fears of being bullied or what the bullies would do to me next. I just carried on day by day trying to keep out of the way of trouble. Little did I know what was about to happen.

I didn't know that behind-the-scenes Mum had started writing to a man in the RAF. In 1949, their relationship developed and later that year I was told to meet my new stepdad. His name was William Thirde, and I was then known as Colin Thirde for part of my life. He had been brought up in a hard Scottish orphanage and to me was as tough as they come. My relationship with William made me feel ill at ease. I think he reminded me of the bullies at school. Alan took the arrival of William very badly. He didn't feel important anymore. His job as head of the house was over and that made him feel isolated.

In winter, there was a lot of snow on the ground and he came out to play snowballs with us. Whenever I got hit by one of his snowballs, I cried. His snowballs were filled with small stones; they really hurt. I was told to toughen up.

On one occasion I was having a bath, when William came in with a bar of carbolic soap and a heavy bristled scrubbing brush and started scrubbing me hard; this was painful and upset me.

Another time I was washing my face when William came up behind me. He bent down and lifted my legs in the air. He held my face underwater. I panicked. I struggled to get air to breathe. He said he would make a man of me. I now have a fear of water. This means that I keep away from any areas of water such as the river and bulrushes at Cranford Woods.

When William was discharged from the Royal Air Force, he left with £800. This was a severance payment for his service. Mum wanted to buy our house but William did not agree. They argued, he lost his temper and he hit her. She asked William why he had hit her. He said, "That's what you do when women argue."

Mum said, "Not with me," and punched him in the face. The shock of being thumped by a woman worked and he never did it again. In that era, a woman should know her place, never to argue with her husband. The man is the dominant person in marriage or any other relationship. Children should be seen and not heard.

Mum was still making us do the household chores; each of us had a list of jobs to do. Jean had to clean the cutlery and I had to clean out the coal fire. The ash had to be taken out into the garden and put on the flowerbeds. The fire then had to be remade for when it was next needed.

Another worry I had on a regular basis was Mum's favourite radio programme, *Mrs Dale's Diary*. It was on at 11am and again at 4.15pm every day. While it was on, I had to stand up straight, next to her chair. I was not to move, cough or sneeze. If I did any of these, she would slap me and say I had ruined her programme.

I did make a couple of friends, one called Alan and one called Ryan. We got on well for a couple of years. We all got an invite to go to Reggie Mewley's Fireworks Night party.

Fireworks Night is a celebration of an attempt to blow up the Houses of Parliament by a man known as Guy Fawkes. Bonfires are lit and people gather round to let off fireworks. They also have hot drinks or beer and eat hot dogs and crisps. This tradition dates back many years. Reggie was the only kid whose parents could afford fireworks. He was a real show-off. He had a very large box of fireworks that somebody (not me) dropped a match into. What happened next was spectacular. The box and fireworks blew up and rockets went in all directions. There was the sound of bangs and explosions from the fireworks. Reggie was trying to find out who did it, but nobody knew and nobody would own up. Everybody went home laughing.

Every Saturday, Jean, Alan and I had to go to Hayes town from Crowland Avenue to do the shopping. It was over a mile away; we had to walk there and back over a big hill which covered the train station. We had to walk past rows of houses close to the main road. We also noticed what was left of the many bombed-out factories. Sometimes, we would stop at the top of the hill near the entrance to the station. We once saw a very fast train. It was called an express train. Other people watching said it was the *Flying Scotsman* from Paddington station travelling at 100 miles an hour. The amount of steam coming from the train caused a fog over the bridge and across the road. The combination of the steam and the vibration from the train caused me to fall over. I was not hurt. I had not seen a train of this size before. When I got to my feet, I could see that the steam was beginning to disperse and we continued on towards the town to do the shopping. Mum gave us a shopping list, with the ration book and the money needed. The list included meat, tea, sugar, butter, milk, dripping, bread and condensed milk. The amount we could have was determined by our ration book. The money Mum gave us was for the chicken food. It was all right going to town but hard work coming back with all the heavy shopping. We would carry the shopping bags between us, each holding one handle of the bag. Mum said that when we got to the top of the road, we must cross in a certain place. We didn't do it, as we thought she wouldn't see us. We didn't know she would sit in the bedroom watching from the window, to catch us out. We were punished for disobeying her when we got home. We were all smacked and scolded for not doing what we were told.

CHAPTER TWO

Colin – Teenage Years (13–19 years)

We next moved to 21 Blythe Road in Hayes town, which was totally different from both Crowland Avenue and Harmondsworth. These were both small villages in the countryside. Hayes town was more industrial and modern. There were shops everywhere, with factories and other businesses. If you were in town at lunchtime or teatime when the factories were rotating shifts, you would see hundreds of cyclists leaving work. It was hard to believe so many people rode bikes. All the roads were pretty congested with the large Castrol depot in the adjacent Clayton Road. There were plenty of small shops and a café near the newsagent's. When you left Clayton Road, you joined the main road, with the town to the left and the railway station up the large hill to the right. On the corner of Clayton Road was a public house called the Railway Arms and a bus stop for a number of buses which went to various destinations. There was the Grand Union Canal which flowed across the main road, under what was called the canal bridge. The canal went to a town called Southall. From the railway station, you could see the giant Nestlé factory, the Kraft cheese building and the Quaker Oats factory, where I once worked for a short time. Back in Hayes there were many bus routes; one passed Hayes Football Club, another went along the Uxbridge Road past Townfield School. In the town the buses were what we called normal, but the buses on the Uxbridge Road, going to London one way, or to Hillingdon the other, were called trolleybuses. These buses had two long poles on the roof which were attached to overhead power cables. Occasionally, these poles came away from the power lines and the bus was stuck in the middle of the road, causing gridlock, which

HAYES STATION

(hand-drawn map)

- RAILWAY STATION
- RAILWAY BRIDGE ENTRANCE
- BUS STOP
- STATION ROAD
- SUBWAY TO STATION
- KINGS ENGINEERING
- BUS STOP   BUS STOP
- E.M.I.
- BLYTHE ROAD
- DUR HOUSE
- BLYTHE ROAD
- CLARENDON ROAD
- BUS STOP
- PUB / NEWS AGENT
- BUS STOP
- SHOPS
- SHOPS   CLAYTON ROAD
- CASTROL DEPOT
- BUS STOP RAILWAY ARCHES
- HAYES TOWN

most people found mildly amusing. The road out of Hayes town to the Uxbridge Road was called Coldharbour Lane. As it passed the school, it came to the Uxbridge Road traffic lights, with St Christopher's Approved School to the right-hand side. Across the road was the local landmark, a public house called the Grapes.

In the move to Hayes town, my life changed. I found myself with no friends AGAIN. This was about the 1950s.

My new school was Townfield School. I started in the juniors and settled in well but then I moved to the seniors and I got bullied again. I was even scared of some teachers. I was told to stand in the corner of the class while the head girl and another girl taught me my times tables. These were basic multiplication tables that every child had to learn and be able to recite from memory. To get round the bullies, who waited till lunch to threaten me, I found a mate who had a bike. He would let me use it at lunchtime. I would ride out of the school till lessons restarted. As time went by, I started playing football and cricket during the lunch break and nobody bothered me. Mum bought me a bike. It made me happy. It meant I could go out most weekends and holidays. Jean and I joined a youth club, and we met new friends. Our neighbour Mrs Swan gave me a football. I went to the park and joined up with a lads' team. I somehow always got a game. I wasn't the best player but I owned the ball. Later in life, I even played for the local working men's club, where I scored my first goal. It made the local papers the next day.

After a couple of years, Mum allowed us more freedom; she let us go to the fairground. Alan was to look after us. We played a joke on him, and hid so he could not find us. Jean and I realised we should not have done this. We went in search of him but had no luck. Eventually, we gave up, thinking that maybe he had gone home. When we got home, he wasn't there. Sometime later, he came home in tears and Mum went berserk at him and hit him on the head with a saucepan. Alan cycled away and was missing for a few days. We were kept inside as punishment and only occasionally allowed out to work in the garden.

Mum had started to read the *Psychic News* as she was interested in spiritualism. She received a copy every week and read it thoroughly.

At this time, we also had comics to read, mainly *The Beano, The Dandy* and *The Eagle,* and sometimes *Film Fun*.

Mum said we were going to have a séance; she told us to sit round the table. We had to put our hands on the table with our fingers stretched out. Each finger had to touch the next person's finger and connect to make a complete circle. We had to sing songs to contact the dead. We had to do this in a darkened room and we had to remain silent while Mum went into a trance to listen for voices from the dead being contacted. We never heard any voices, but Mum was convinced that the spirits were present. Afterwards, she suggested we should go to the spiritualist hall in Hayes town to further our experience. It was interesting; we did not know what was supposed to happen, and we never went again.

Jean and I were close as brother and sister. Looking back at our early years, life was not a bed of roses. There were bad times, good times and frightening times, but to us it was what it was. What did we know! We couldn't even think anything was wrong. Moving to Hayes was a learning curve. I was allowed out on my own and every Saturday I went to watch Hayes Football Club. Hayes played in the Athenian league. Their ground was called Church Road. I have followed Hayes FC since I was young and admired the skills of legendary players such as Stan 'soapy' Hudson, Les Champelovier and Derek Neate, who later broke his leg in a match. I really loved going to the matches and I have followed the team through thick and thin to this day.

I found my relationship with William was slowly improving, and he did not mind me calling him Willie. At 21 Blythe Road, Hayes, we had a large, long garden. We grew our own vegetables, including potatoes, which were plentiful. Mum, Jean and I did the digging. Alan also helped. We kept chickens. I gathered the eggs they laid and cleaned off the droppings board, which was slotted in under their roost. I then had to take the board to the compost heap and clean the droppings off the board before replacing it under the roost; a horrible, smelly job.

Willie got a job at Electrical Musical Industries, EMI for short. This was at the top of Blythe Road so his job was close to home. This was a large building which included recording studios and vinyl productions for Britain's best singers and musicians. On the other side of the road there was a building that made parts for various pieces of musical equipment for EMI and further afield.

I also got my first Saturday job delivering meat. I spent my Saturdays riding the firm's bike with the meat stacked in the front basket. My deliveries took me to various parts of Hayes and surrounding districts. This took most of the morning and I got a few tips. In the afternoon I was told to burn the rubbish out in the yard. I had to collect bits of broken wooden crates, disused paper and cardboard boxes which had mounted up over the week. There was quite a pile. All the rubbish was put in the concrete-covered yard and I got the fire started. It eventually got so fierce that it caused the concrete to explode and it bubbled up the paint on the garage doors. I got the sack.

With my new-found friends at football, I felt wanted again. I was aware that some of the boys were not nice but I had to keep my end up. We did silly things, like going to the pictures without tickets. One lad would pay to go in and open the side door for the rest of us to sneak in. We did this a lot. Sometimes, the police would be called, but we always got away.

It was around this time that I met my first girlfriend, a girl called Anne. In a short space of time we met often and went for long walks together. I had never had any thoughts about girls before this time; I had certainly never met any. On this day, as Anne and I walked by some garages, she went over to one and leant against the door. She unbuttoned her blouse and put my hand inside. I had no idea what she was doing, I was really scared. I removed my hand from her blouse and legged it. I was confused for days but could not confide in anyone, least of all my family. I did meet Anne a few times after my first experience and eventually became fully educated in the finer arts of passion. We managed to flatten grass in many places without getting into trouble.

Alan got his call-up papers from the army. Alan did his basic training at Catterick Army Camp in Yorkshire. After training, Alan's job was as a batman to an officer. He found life very difficult in the army and could not cope at all, which led to him spending some of his army life in the guardhouse. He did not come to terms with authority or the routine of army life, which brought about his early discharge. Alan would never discuss his experiences with any of the family and after his short spell in the army this was no different. He would not confide in anyone.

After he came home, Alan often cycled to many different places, mainly for peace of mind. Alan was quite a secretive person. When he came home, he would occasionally say the name of a town or county he had cycled through, but would give no details. He once said he had cycled to the Devon coast and had slept rough on the journey. This we found out many years later.

As time went on, I got a full-time job selling eggs from baskets at the local grocer's. They were not nice – cracked and smelly, just like the aroma from the droppings board, I remember, in the garden at home. The grocer's was called Goodworths. I worked there for some time. Jean also worked there as an assistant behind the counter serving the public, with a couple of other girls. The shop manager was called Mr Wilson, Tug for short. He stayed in the back of the shop checking the deliveries and sorting out the stock. The staff did not like him very much because he was full of his own importance.

After the earlier instances at the pictures with my friends, I started to go again every week but it was different this time. I paid at the desk for every film I watched. I sat in the 9d front seats. The middle seats were 1 shilling and 3d, the rear seats were 3 shillings and 6d. The circle was more expensive; we never sat up there. In Hayes, there were many local picture houses. They were called the Ambassador, the Savoy, the Essoldo and the Gaumont, I even went to the Fleapit in West Ealing. I loved watching comedy films; there were plenty of them. They starred Laurel and Hardy, the Marx Brothers, Abbott and Costello, the Bowery Boys and Norman Wisdom. I developed a liking for musicals and watched a lot at this time. I also loved westerns. I have seen almost every western film made in that era.

It was around that time that I met Pauline. She became my regular girlfriend and we were together for a long time, never apart. We went to the pictures to see *Rock Around the Clock,* which followed the release of an American record of the same name featuring Bill Haley and his Comets. The film was an introduction of many artists that were performing a different type of music, later to be known as rock and roll. Some of the artists in the film would become household names in the future, including the Platters and Freddie Bell and the Bell Boys, amongst many others. The music had a beat that was easy to dance to and many other artists followed, writing their own versions. This style of music and dance came to be a British sensation which would last for many years. Eventually, names like Tommy Steele, Adam Faith and later Cliff Richard and the Shadows would become pop icons of the future. At one stage, there were more up-and-coming singers than there were songs for them to sing. I had heard that at least three up-and-coming singers were arguing outside the venue about who was going to sing each song. I want to pay tribute to the first British singer that I heard. His name was Terry Dene, and he was the first singer to make famous the song *Stairway of Love*. Without this man, rock and roll in this country would not have taken off so quickly. It opened the door for a worldwide change in popular music. It was the experience of my life: cinema patrons were dancing in the aisles and on the stage. People were even dancing in the streets. The police could not stop them; it changed life from the Victorian era to the modern day way of life. I was hooked.

I still look back at my life when I was at school. Thinking about the time I hid my schoolbooks, mainly mathematics and English, in my desk. I was easily distracted in class and didn't put my books out for marking when told to do so. I was scared of being punished if I got the answers wrong. However, the teacher noticed my books were missing and looked for them in my desk. I was punished. The teacher knew I wrote with my right hand so I held out my left hand, for a ruler turned on its edge. He brought it down across the back of my fingers. It hurt so much that I could hardly grip anything. Mum said that if I got punished at school, it was my fault. She would back up the school by punishing me at home as well.

Enjoying my teen years out in the world, things were not right at home. Mum and Willie were not getting on; they were rowing a lot. I had collected my violin from school, having started lessons. I was practising in the lounge when a row broke out. I tried to play *There is a Happy Land*, which made them both laugh and lifted the tension for a while. Things didn't really change in the long run. My relationship with Willie had improved. He didn't tell Mum he caught me riding my bike like an idiot. He told me quietly to behave. I was grateful.

As we got older, Alan, Jean and I all got jobs in Hayes. Alan at Coppen's grocer's, Jean at a sweet shop called Lavells, and Willie got me a job with EMI – the same place where he was working. My first wage was 3 shillings, and 6 old pennies an hour – £7.14 per week – which was taken by Mum, as was Jean's, Alan's and Willie's. She gave us very little back, saying the rest was for board and keep.

Later, I heard about the death of the King, George VI. The King's funeral procession by train passed through Hayes station, towards Paddington. I joined a few hundred people lining the station, also standing on the bridge. There was a mix of emotions. Some stood silently; some were quietly shedding a tear; many were sobbing out loud. Most people bowed their heads in respect as the train passed. Alan went to see him lying in state in the capital, with thousands of other mourners. It was a historic event. We learnt later that Princess Elizabeth would access the throne in due course.

As time went on, Pauline and I went our separate ways. We both wanted different things, which was good news for her dad. He didn't really like me, or any other boy she went out with. I often spent a lot of time riding my bike around the town. I noticed another boy riding near to me. I was aware he was close by, almost like he seemed to want a race. We did race. It ended in a draw as our wheels passed the marker we'd agreed on at the very same time. He told me his name was Ben and he lived with his dad. We became good friends and cycled to many places. We went up to Windsor every Sunday. All the girls we met fancied us. We hired a canoe and paddled up the Thames. We laughed and joked; these were great days with the girls. We had a lot of fun. My other pastime was playing cards. I did this quite a lot; not for money but for matchsticks. We found another friend this way. He was called Eddie and his parents joined in when we played cards.

Ben and I kept cycling and I still played cards. Ben sold his bicycle and bought a motorbike. I was a bit nervous at first as this was a new experience for me. I had never ridden on a motorbike. I was not used to travelling at speed and it wasn't any easier for me sitting behind the driver. I soon realised that I had to lean with the bike as it moved in and out of traffic and round corners to balance the bike. In time, I learnt to cope with the movement of the bike to help the driver manoeuvre. This turned out to be good for us both.

Back home, things hadn't improved. Part of the tension stemmed from Mum saying that no one ever visited us. We never brought any friends home because we were nervous about what reception they would get. I suggested to Mum that I would bring a few mates round. This helped to ease the situation. Ben arrived with a couple of girls. Mum had made a sponge cake, some jam tarts and drinks, which were all very nice. We talked all afternoon and things went well. It did not change the atmosphere at home.

A few days later, Ben told me his brother John was home on leave. He wanted me to meet him, which I did. He was a nice guy, and he spoke about life in the RAF. He enjoyed the variety of activities, the chance to learn a trade and the opportunity to travel round the world, meeting all kinds of people. I found this very appealing and could see myself escaping from home to live a new life in peace. After mulling this over and talking to Ben and John, the idea cemented in my mind that I wanted to try this. A few days later, I dropped the bombshell to the family that I wanted to join the RAF. You could hear a pin drop in the room. Nothing was said; I could see the red mist in Mum's face. I had made my mind up; it was time to go. Mum said no and called me ungrateful, reminding me of all the things she'd done for me. She was in a raging temper and at one point went to hit me. So I ran to the back door. As I went out, she threw a handful of knives and forks at me. I was so scared that I jumped over the garden gate and ran.

I went straight to Eddie's house and his parents agreed to put me up for a couple of nights. I explained to Eddie and his parents what had happened. I was pleasantly surprised that Eddie and his parents listened to me, and I felt relaxed in their company. The home was peaceful, with no rowing or tension in the air. We even spent time playing a few rounds of cards and laughing at a few jokes before having a good night's sleep. We spent a lot of time talking through my situation. It was decided that I had to do what was right for me. After being away for a couple of days, I had plucked up enough courage to go back home. Mum let me in, there was a wall of silence

– Mum would not speak to me. A few days passed before Mum finally broke the silence. She asked me if I had changed my mind. I told her that I hadn't. Willie was also there and asked where I had got the idea from. I told him it was because John was talking to me about his life in the services. I also reminded Willie that he was in the RAF himself. Willie and Mum talked it over and finally agreed, but on one condition: I had to take up nursing. I was horrified at the thought, but if that was the only way, I had to say "Yes." I went to the RAF recruitment centre in Acton for an interview. I was successful and passed the tests required to attend the recruitment camp. I was eighteen years old.

Colin in the Airforce.

I got my rail pass to Bedford and was met by RAF personnel and driven to the recruits' camp at Cardington in Bedfordshire. The camp was large and comprised of accommodation called billets for regular airmen and facilities for those personnel who had arrived from various recruitment centres. There was a dance party arranged at the weekend for male and female recruits. An event designed to help new entrants to socialise and relax in their new surroundings. On Monday morning, we attended a group gathering. We were quickly told that we had a week in which to decide whether to sign up or to leave and return home. I signed up at the end of the week. We travelled from Cardington to our respective camps. Mine was in West Kirby in Liverpool for square bashing. I settled in well.

I was self-conscious, not knowing what to do, and admit to

suffering an inferiority complex. I felt anxious in the new surroundings and always thought I was not good enough to be in any situation. This stems from my childhood at home where I was always told by Mum that I would not be good at anything and that the only friends I would have I would have to buy rather than get on merit. I could not go into the station NAAFI, as I felt everybody was looking at me. The NAAFI was a meeting place for all personnel, where you could discuss the day's events. There was also a canteen for food and drinks. You could also listen to records on the jukebox. I did make some friends at the camp and managed to find a girlfriend.

Between all the drills, coping with getting up at 5.30am and kit cleaning, etc., things went quite well. I played football and did cross-country running, which took me away from marching. Unfortunately, on one occasion, the drill corporal asked me why I hadn't kept up with my marching. I panicked and said I'd missed my periods, instead of saying I was cross-country running. You can imagine the laughter from other airmen; I never lived it down. For a long time all the lads were asking now how my periods were, and some asked if I needed a few days in bed. I had even managed to get sympathetic looks from the Women's Royal Air Force (WRAF) personnel, along with a few giggles.

After eight weeks' training, we were all given postings; mine being Central Medical Establishments (CME for short) in Great Portland Street in London. This was a large building at the bottom of Great Portland Street near to Edgeware Road. There was a basement and three further floors. The basement was used for storage, including my bike which I rode to work on. I rode from Hayes each day as this position was classed as a home posting. The ground floor was the reception area. The first floor was used for officers' medicals and records. The second floor was the telephone exchange, which was manned seven days a week, twenty-four hours.

I arrived at CME with my kitbag from Great Portland Street station, to find a lot of policemen and reporters with photographers at the entrance to the building. I was stopped at the door by police. I had to explain who I was and where I was going before they let me go inside. As I went to the lift, I saw a very pretty blonde-haired girl in the foyer. I went to the first floor and asked the sergeant what was going on. He said the lady was Ruth Ellis (the last woman to be hung). She had to have a medical to make sure she was fit to be hung! This seemed very odd to me. She obviously passed her medical; she was hung a couple of days later. I believe this happened at Pentonville Prison by the then hangman Albert Pierrepoint. He was later known as the King of Swing.

My job at CME was to accompany pilots from civil aviation, along with RAF pilots, to various doctors for their medicals. This became a very busy duty, as each pilot had to go to numerous doctors for various tests, before completing the full medical and being cleared to fly. One of my last duties at CME was to take a civilian pilot to have his medical. His name was Captain Thain, the pilot on the ill-fated Manchester United plane, which crashed at Munich Airport. I was at CME for about eighteen months, before being posted to RAF Halton – a large air force hospital, officer cadets' and musicians' training centre at Wendover in Buckinghamshire.

Before reporting to Halton, I went home on leave. Alan had moved to Devon and got a job there. Jean was at home. I went to see some old friends; I met up with Ben and we talked about my life in the RAF. I played football with other friends.

I settled in at Halton; it was different to CME. It was a very busy hospital for RAF personnel. I went to medical classes every day but was not interested in passing my trade test or being a nurse. It wasn't rocket science that I did not pass, though I didn't tell Mum. There would be hell to pay! I wondered why she was so keen for me to be a doctor. This I found out many years later.

One of the first activities involved a lesson for nurses to work in a wartime situation. I was put into the cockpit of a fake crashed plane. The nurses were supposed to get me out. I was meant to yell in pain. I didn't do this because I was so intrigued by the controls in the cockpit that I forgot to yell. The officer in charge caught me looking at all the dials and levers. He said he would see me later. Thinking I was in trouble, I went to see him. He told me he was not pleased with my attitude. I said I was only here in the RAF because my mum wouldn't sign my entry form unless I was a nurse. He asked if I would like a transfer to something I wanted to do. He suggested I move to air service rescue. I was over the moon but then remembered I would

Colin – Teenage Years (13–19 years)

have broken my word to Mum, so unfortunately I had to decline.

A couple of weeks later, I had a seventy-two-hour pass, which was to change my life again. When I was due to return, Ben said, "I'll take you back to camp." We were riding up the road towards the camp, going into the last corner on the main road near the hospital, when Ben shouted, "We are off!"

I felt the bike starting to slide. I rolled myself up. I found myself bouncing up the road like a ball. We didn't have crash helmets in those days. When I came to a stop, I remember looking up and seeing a hospital sign with an arrow pointing the way. The next thing I can remember was being in the operating theatre. A nurse who was in my billet came into the theatre, saw it was me and collapsed. I was aware of a loud crash.

My stay in hospital was a long one – with a bad head injury. I was having five injections a day in my backside. It must have looked like a pin cushion. I didn't know what happened to Ben or the bike, or even if he was hurt. I presumed he was all right as he did tell Mum about the accident. Neither Ben nor anyone from the family came to visit me in hospital. After three months in hospital, I got two weeks' leave. I went home; life was never the same. I met up with Ben but the friendship was just about okay. I got on his bike but every time we went round a bend, I fought to stay upright. This made it difficult for Ben to control the bike and he let me know it. Eventually, Ben got friendly with other bikers. Our friendship was slowly coming to an end, but not with any animosity. I just didn't see him again.

I went back to camp but could not work for long periods. I'd worked on the ear, nose and throat ward (ENT) as an orderly for a while. I didn't realise at the time that I wasn't up to the job. A few months later, I went to see a senior nurse and we had a long talk. He said he would discuss our talk with a medical officer. The outcome was a medical discharge from the RAF. I had signed up for nine years but was discharged after three years.

After my discharge, I went home. I told Mum, Willie and Jean about the accident and my discharge. None of my family asked how I was, so life was back to normal. Mum and Willie were still not getting on, so I sought out my old friends. Then came a new bombshell.

CHAPTER THREE

Colin – Mr Casino Twenties (21–32 years)

Unbeknown to me, Mum had befriended a woman she had got to know. She told the family this lady had offered to help her buy a house, and that we were moving in a few weeks. We were all shocked. Jean and Willie had to leave their jobs and were not happy. Mum said we were moving to Burnley in Lancashire some 200 miles away. I travelled in the moving lorry; the family got a train. When I got to Burnley, the house was awful; no garden, gas lighting and an ancient brick outside toilet. I thought it was a dump.

Colin – Mr Casino Twenties (21–32 years)

I don't know what Jean and Willie thought. I thought here we go again, no friends. However – Mum was happy. It was 1960; I was twenty-two years old. I thought I'd gone back thirty years. Where the heck was I? I'd never seen terraced housing. I had to get used to coming out of my front door straight onto the street; it was a nightmare. The neighbours were very friendly. They brought us tea and cakes when we were moving in. They told us about the area. They also told us about a man with a long pole with a piece of metal on the end, who came down the road knocking on people's bedroom windows to wake them up. Our house was about three bus stops from the town centre; the fare was 2 old pennies.

At first, I slept in the sitting room on the sofa because we had not unpacked fully. In the morning, Willie came into the sitting room. He flung open the front door wide and all the windows. I was really comfortable. I could not wake up. When I did come round, I could smell gas. Apparently, when I went to bed, while I was undressing, I pulled my jumper over my head and hadn't realised I'd broken the gas mantle on the gas light, so gas had been escaping all night. The gas light was in the middle of the room, but the ceilings were far lower in these houses. Willie saved me from a sticky end. I'd never seen gas lighting in a house before.

In the meantime, Jean and Mum set about making the house liveable. Mum loved decorating. She decorated every house we lived in; there were plenty of them. This first house in Burnley was in Branch Road, before we moved on to Hufling Lane, which was a better house.

This house was near the grounds of the famous Towneley Hall, which attracts thousands of people from all over the world every year to see the magnificent stately home and surrounding estate, which consists of a vast amount of open land. Part of the land was used for football pitches by local teams. A large wooded area, home to various species of birds and other wildlife. Photographers and twitchers come to enjoy the peace of the woodland. There is a large pond in front of the main house with a spectacular water feature and an abundance of ducks, again many species. There is also a large golf course for amateur golfers to take part in tournaments and after games visit the 19th hole.

A few days later, I decided to take a trip down town. I was quietly taken with the surroundings. I was amazed to see the trams, unlike living in Hayes where we had trolleybuses. Another sight was seeing many people covered in coal dust; they were miners. There were many coal mines in the area. Part of the town was undergoing modernisation. There was a very large circle near the town centre covered in mud, which was going to be a large roundabout. Further on, they were building a posh hotel called the Keirby Hotel. There was the Palace Picture House, with a market behind it. I found a café called The 47. I spent a lot of time at The 47 café. It seemed a good place for making friends. I found the people were very friendly, unlike in London, where you hardly knew your neighbours. At The 47 café, I got to meet a couple of boys. They offered to take me on a tour of the area. We drove for miles. We went to a lot of country pubs in the middle of nowhere. Some of the countryside was breathtaking. I was beginning to enjoy myself. I decided that it was time to look for work. I got a good position at Woodside old folks' home. I was to replace the man in charge of the men's section, who was leaving. I did split shifts with some afternoons off. I also got a job at the local Wimpy bar. The Wimpy bar was all the rage in the sixties. It attracted young people who wanted a place to be together. It served burgers (called Wimpys), tea, coffee and soft drinks. I cooked the Wimpys and I once cooked 300 Wimpys in one afternoon. I loved it! The management liked me at the Wimpy bar. The Wimpy bar was next to the Palace bingo hall (formerly the picture house). I got an evening job as a bingo ticket checker. I now had three jobs and a girlfriend. Jean got a job at the Mecca bingo hall – our opposition. Willie got a job at a local factory. Everything was going well for now.

I would like to add that I am writing this book at the ripe old age of eighty-three. Today, I have learnt of the death of Her Majesty Queen Elizabeth II, who has passed away at Balmoral Castle in Scotland. Today, it is the 8th of September 2022. Two years after the death of her husband, the Duke of Edinburgh; she was ninety-six and he was ninety-nine. They will be sorely missed. Her eldest son will be known as King Charles III.

Ten days later, we watched the Queen's State Funeral, which was the largest state funeral in history. The funeral of Queen Elizabeth was a full day of events. The procession of the coffin went through the streets of London, with regiments from all the services present in ceremonial dress. Britain excels at ceremonial occasions with unrivalled precision. The public lined the route. Many millions wanting to pay their respects to the monarch. The service was at Westminster Abbey and was attended by dignitaries from all over the world. After the service, the funeral cortege made its way from London to Windsor Castle. The hearse was specially designed with windows to all sides, lower than usual, so that people from all directions could see the coffin. When the cortege arrived in Windsor, it drove up the long walk at Windsor Castle before entering the courtyard of the castle, where the Queen's favourite horse, Emma and two Corgies were waiting. Another service followed in Windsor Castle in St George's Chapel, after which the Queen's coffin was lowered to rest next to the Duke of Edinburgh. I watched the whole proceedings with Gillian, my wife. It was a historic day to witness. It was important to both of us to honour the Queen's life.

While getting to know the local people and places, I was told Burnley FC was just up the road. I couldn't wait to get there. I hadn't been to a match since I left Hayes. It brought back memories of my early years when I played in the ruins of bombed and burnt-down factories – of which there were plenty. My relationship with Willie had improved. We went to the match every Saturday. He was a hard, stubborn Scotsman. We stood on the terraces. On one occasion, hooligans at the top of the terraces were throwing proper metal darts down on the people below. I said, "Let's move to a safer place."

He said, "I'm happy here, I'm not moving." Luckily, we were not hurt.

Another occasion saw Jean and I entering a dance competition. It was run by the Senior Service cigarette company. Each couple had to dance the jive. We came third. We won a large packet of cigarettes, which was very good; neither Jean nor I smoked. We were pleased we had entered and even more so to be placed. I still went to The 47 and regularly went out with my friends. I still had my three jobs. My life was about to change, yet again, in a very big way.

I had heard about a southern company called Thanet and Kent who wanted to put gaming into the bingo hall at night after bingo had finished. I heard they wanted to train croupiers. I applied. Little did I know that more than 200 others had also applied. Amazingly, I was one of those accepted. That was the end of my cooking career at this time and my work at the old folks' home. I told Mum what I'd done. Needless to say, she went absolutely berserk, calling me all the names under the sun. She hardly spoke to me for several days. I could see she was upset. I didn't know why, other than she thought gaming was not a career that she wanted me to be in. She felt it was a den of iniquity.

In the bingo hall, the gaming tables that were set up were blackjack tables. We had to practise dealing, with the Thanet and Kent staff posing as the punters. I started my first bit of dealing, but there was a small problem: I could not shuffle the cards. I tried but shuffled in blocks of ten or twelve. I kept on trying but to no avail. The boss of the company was an American, who I didn't know was watching me in the seats upstairs in the bingo hall through his binoculars. He said to me later, "If you can't shuffle by the weekend, you are out of here."

Every night, I sat up in bed trying to shuffle the cards. I tried all night; I had to get it right. All of a sudden, the cards were slipping out of my hand. I caught them; I knew how to control the cards. The weekend came when I started to shuffle. I did it perfectly! I turned to see if the boss was watching and he was. I treated him to an enormous V sign from my table. Afterwards, he sent for me. He said that no one had ever done that to him before –don't do it again. I kept my job. He could see that I was determined and that I was trying to do the job properly.

Some nights when I was not working, a few lads and I went to a house to play cards. Nothing serious, just for a few pounds here and there. One of the players – whom I wasn't keen on – kept looking at me, though he never spoke a word. A few days later, I went home. Mum said that a man had called asking for me. She asked, "Who's that greasy man? You must know him."

I knew who she was talking about. It was the bloke who kept staring at me. Mum said, "He wants to speak to you. What have you done?"

I said, "Nothing."

His name was Bob. Mum said, "You want to stay away from him. He doesn't look like a very nice man." I didn't know what she meant. I did go to see him. Yet again, my life changed considerably.

He said he was opening a casino. He wanted to employ me as a blackjack dealer. I said, "No." I just did not like him.

He came to me a few days later. He said, "Come to my club. If you don't like what you see, I won't bother you again." I had nothing to lose. I went and what a shock I got. The club was stunning and the cabaret was great, so I moved to his club.

The club was called The 77 Club. It was named after an American television series called *77 Sunset Strip*. The club was housed in an old warehouse, which had previously been used for dancing and roller skating. Jean and I went a couple of times and jived to rock and roll records being played by an enthusiast. As I stepped into what was now The 77 Club, I could hardly take in the transformation. It was a large oblong building. It now had a bar near the entrance. The floor was covered with a beautiful plush carpet, which extended right though up to the stage at the far end. The stage had room for the club's organ and drum kit and the microphones were placed at the front, ready for the cabaret. Between the bar and the stage, tables and chairs were set out for the audience. There was further seating to the sides, which was slightly higher than the main floor. The gaming room was at the back behind the stage, partitioned from the main area. The decoration in the casino was stunning, with long velvet orange drapes from floor to ceiling. It was also carpeted. There were two blackjack tables, two roulette tables and a very large *chemin de fer* table. This was a game only for high-stakes players.

On my first night at The 77 Club, it was absolutely packed. The place was buzzing. The compère, who introduced the artists, was called Sam. There was a singer, then an acrobat and another act to close the first half of the show. A forty-five-minute interval followed to let people get drinks, use the toilets and visit the gaming room. The tables were busy and the customers could place small bets, in old money; half a crown, 5 shillings, and bigger stakes, up to £5 limit. The gaming continued through the second half of the cabaret and on into the night after the show had finished. I had made a very good debut on the tables. My new boss said I had done well, which made me feel good as I had also made a winning start. I settled into my new career very quickly.

I have a habit of putting my foot in it, when I do things without thinking. On one occasion at The 77 Club in Brierfield, near Burnley, exotic dancers (strippers) were on stage, as were the (blue) comedians before and during the gaming. I had arrived at the club just before the show was about to begin. I selected what I thought was a nice quiet out-of-the-way table where I could read my Sunday paper in peace. I wasn't watching the show but was aware of a woman coming towards me. She asked, "Is there something wrong with you?" She went on: "It was rude of you to be reading a paper while I am performing." I apologised but pointed out that she hadn't got anything I'd not seen before. She swore at me and left. I finished my paper and started work. Over a period of time I often sat and had a cup of tea with the girls and found them not as some people thought, which brings me to my second clanger.

I didn't drink alcohol before the gaming started, always a cup of tea from the little tea bar in the gaming room. On this Sunday I went for my cuppa and the only person drinking tea was a man I didn't know. He said to me, "Aren't you going to watch the stripper?"

I said, "Do me a favour. Have you seen the one on now?"

He said, "That's my wife."

I waited for the ground to swallow me up, or even a punch on the nose, but luckily for me, he said, "Don't worry, mate. No offence taken." It was then I learnt to keep my mouth shut. You never know who you are talking to.

I soon decided to take driving lessons. I had taken lessons while living in Hayes, but as everyone knows, teenagers do stupid things. So when I took my test I didn't cover myself in glory. My instructor told me to be careful with my examiner as she was a bit strict. I was used to that with Mum. He told me to say "Good afternoon," open the passenger side door, then ask if she was comfortable. I did what I was told, but she just got in and didn't say a word, I thought that was rude.

As we went along, she said, "We are going to do an emergency stop, so when I move my hand, stop the car as quickly and carefully as you can, without skidding." As soon as she finished talking, she

Colin – Mr Casino Twenties (21–32 years)

bashed the dashboard. It made me jump! She said, "That's no good. Do it again." This time, I was ready. As soon as she raised her hand, I slammed on the brake. She shot out of her seat and hit the dashboard hard! She was not happy. She failed me on the spot. I thought, that'll sort her out. I did not drive again for some time after that. I was now ready to take up driving lessons again seriously.

Bob had opened a few more casinos – another two in Burnley, one in Blackburn and another in Doncaster. My new driving instructor was another croupier who liked a drink. When we worked together, he would come and pick me up from my home, then I would drive to the casino and back home. He would drop me off then drive to his home. He didn't charge me; it was a good deal for both of us. He got me through my test with no problems. I got my pass and I bought my first car.

Things had not improved at home. Mum and Willie's marriage was still strained. Jean had changed jobs and was now working at the Mecca ballroom. We had moved house again and we all set about the redecorating. I couldn't do a lot as I was away a lot with my job. Alan had got married and came to live in Barnoldswick. We didn't see much of him because Mum didn't like his wife. She didn't hide it, so he stayed away.

When I got my first car, it was okay. Then I spotted what I thought was a better one, but it wasn't. I kept on changing cars until I got the right one. The trouble was, they were all worse bone-shakers than I had before. The local garage owners were always pleased to see me. It was like, here he comes again, let's get rid of this one.

One car I bought was my pride and joy: a mark 9 Jaguar. I thought this was it! I felt like the bee's knees driving along. Then one of my mates said, "Nice car, but did you know the front is 1963 and the back part is 1959?" My jaw dropped. I knew it had a bit of a rattle, but I didn't care. I got another car from a reputable dealer. All was well, this time no more changing cars.

When Mum saw I had a decent car, she stepped in. She wanted me to take her to see people she knew, also take her shopping. I had to pick up Jean from work, as well as Willie from his work. I felt like a taxi driver. I took Mum to Cleveleys when she went away for a week with Jean. I didn't argue; it kept the peace.

I was doing well as a croupier. Every time Bob bought a new club, I went to it to start up the gambling. I wanted to be the best croupier. I worked hard to get to the top. I practised every night to memorise card sequences and to learn systems. I needed this expertise as some of the punters were not too honest. I learnt to stack cards but only to stop crooks beating me. There were quite a lot of crooks and they would take pleasure in beating the croupier at his own game. I was self-taught at cards and was proud of my achievement. I reached a stage where I would go to the club one hour before the cabaret started. I stood at the bar watching everybody who came in. I didn't want to be caught out by any dodgy gamblers. It taught me to study people closely. I learnt quickly who was genuine and who wasn't.

Many years later, I still do this. I'm not the trusting type. I need to know a person a long time before trusting them. There are a few exceptions. I've learnt that confidence is the greatest asset of life and dress the greatest disguise of life. This has become a guiding principle throughout my life. Mum always told me the most trustworthy people were ex-military officers and people of high rank, to which I replied that the jails are full of them. They are called con men. As usual, my comment didn't go down very well.

During my croupier days, I learnt how to operate roulette tables and other games, but the game to be the dealer of was *chemin de fer*. To deal at this game was the icing on the cake. There were not many clubs who had it in their casinos. I felt honoured to be asked to do it. It is a high-stakes game. It was featured in the James Bond film *Doctor No*. I have worked in many casinos – at least twenty that I remember – and had a high reputation amongst my colleagues. Most casinos had cabarets. The money made at the tables paid the artists' wages for the week. They were contracted for the week's shows, which usually started on Sunday evening. Before the show started, there was a band call, which started around 4pm. All the artists would go through their routines with the musicians and the compères. At the end, artist and croupiers got to meet each other and go to the local restaurants for lunch. Over the years, I met hundreds of singers, groups and comedians. I studied them all, learning all the jokes and one-liners. I developed a sense of humour, which I have kept up to this day. At the age of eighty-three, I can tell a joke and ad-lib a one-liner every time I get the chance, but never to put anyone down.

It doesn't cost anything to be well-mannered, or to have a smile or laugh, or be respectful. Many of the people I have met were mostly nice, though some were not. I will not name names. One person I met stood out as a real gentleman. He could sing from the back of the stage or any other part of the room, without a microphone. His diction and projection of his voice meant that you could understand the words clearly. His name was Donald Peers, a man of long ago. He would sit and have a cup of tea with you, with no airs or graces. One artist that again stood out, even though he only appeared for one night as a special guest, was the American crooner Johnnie Ray. What an impressive show. There were a lot of young women in the audience. He sang personally to them. One girl at the front came to the edge of the stage. As he bent down to shake her hand, she put her arms round his neck. He lifted her off the floor and onto the stage. They sang a duet. She was not that good, but the performance brought the house down. She wasn't part of the show.

I sat with other croupiers at one club when we had finished for the night. We sat down for a drink, with a group of Irishmen. We had not recognised any of them, but one was Joseph Locke – whom you all would know as a great singer. This was not the Mr X who was impersonating Joseph at local clubs. Joseph had a heated exchange of views with him in Ireland. He was not impressed with this man impersonating him. I don't think he did it again.

Willie got a part-time job at one club that I worked at. I had developed a rather flamboyant way of dealing. This attracted a lot of people who had come into the gaming room in the show's interval. I would see Willie watching me through the crowd. He had a proud look on his face. Shortly after, a man came over and said to me, "How do you deal like that? Would you like to join the Magic Circle?"

I replied, "I'm not that good." Nothing developed from it.

I haven't mentioned that Bob had a brother called Donald, who I got on really well with. I bought his house, on the outskirts of Burnley. It was a lovely place, with open views and a garden full of fruit trees and bushes. We moved yet again. Meanwhile, Bob had what I thought was a silent partner, called Fred. I had seen him a few times over the years. The croupiers were suddenly called to head office during the day. We were told Fred and Bob were splitting up. Fred had a circuit of clubs in Yorkshire. We had to decide who was going with Fred and who was staying with Bob. I chose Fred, as I was desperate to leave home. My new position was to be the manager of the Spa Casino in Harrogate. It was near the Spa Gardens, opposite the Conference Hall.

I went home and told Mum I was going to Harrogate. I had a flat there. As usual, she had a few nasty words to say. I knew she would cut up rough. Shortly after I first became a croupier, another croupier asked me to move into his flat to help with the rent. Mum said, "Is this house not good enough for you, who's going to do your washing and cooking? I suppose you'll have some floozy to do it for you." She created such an atmosphere that I did not move away at that time. Jean had changed her job and moved to kitchenware makers Prestige.

I settled in Harrogate to my new job quite well and got on well with customers. I was aware that things were far from what I thought when I started. A lot of the people were farmers. I sensed there were a lot of undesirables knocking about. Fred and his girlfriend, who I didn't know, often went to the Spa Gardens and played on the putting green. Fred could put away a bottle of Scotch a night but never seemed to be drunk. He was a laid-back man and didn't seem to bother about anything. He did have the ability to sort out trouble. Anyone who started trouble, Fred would get them a glass of whisky. He would ask them to sit down and have a drink, saying let's see what your problem is. It always worked. This attitude saved me from a beating.

One night, a waiter came to me. He said, "There are two men winning a lot of money on the blackjack table." I went to have a look. One man was sitting down; the other was standing behind him. Alarm bells were ringing in my head, so I swapped places with the dealer. I could then have a better idea of what was going on. After a few hands, I was worried. I couldn't find out what they were doing, but they were still winning. I couldn't put in my stacking systems, as I feared they were professional cheats, so drastic action was needed.

I said to the waiter, "Tell those men the manager wants to speak to them." I (the manager) told them, "I am not happy with the way you are playing," knowing full well they would cause trouble. I knew that when I called them out, they would make a scene, which would empty the club. That's what happened.

They shouted, "Call the police. He's called us cheats."

I knew as soon as they yelled police that they had got me. I called the police, which could cause the club to lose its licence. We all went to my office; a constable, a sergeant, the players and myself. Not Fred; he was at his other club in Blackpool. The man (his mate had gone) claimed I didn't like him winning. The constable, bless him, suggested we count the cards. The cards were still on the card table downstairs. I said, "I'll go and get them."

The sergeant said to the constable, "Go with him."

We went and got the cards. As we were about to go up the stairs to my office, I said to the constable, "Please take the cards. It is better if you handle them."

He said, "It's all right, sir. You keep them."

Then suddenly it hit me. Here's my chance. When you go upstairs, you could either walk or use the lift. By the lift was a plastic flower arrangement. We started up the stairs. I held the cards behind my back. While doing that, I palmed a couple of cards off the pack and dropped them onto the flowers. The cards were plastic and slipped out of sight. In the office, I gave the cards to the sergeant, who counted them. The man looked horrified! The policeman asked if I wanted to press charges. I said, "I want to speak to the man alone."

When we were alone, he said, "How did you do that?"

I said, "Do what? But here's the deal: you leave all your winnings on the table and you're free to go."

The deal was done. As he left, he said, "See you soon."

A couple of weeks went by, then one night I noticed two men having a drink and watching me intently. I went to reception and asked, "Who are those men over there, how did they get in?"

The receptionist said, "They told me they were friends of yours."

I wasn't happy with that explanation and said, "I'm not hard to find. You should have come to find me."

As the evening went on, some of the customers left, but these men stayed there until it was just me and them. My heart was pounding;

I thought this was my comeuppance. I went over and asked, "Okay, what's the score?"

One of the men threw a £5 casino chip on the table and said, "My boss sent this."

Then his mate piped up and said, "I know you. You once worked at the Wilton Club in Manchester".

I said yes. What a dump that casino was. I'd worked there for Bob. He was trying to get a gaming concession there. I did three nights; it was horrible and rough.

One of the men stood up and said, "Fred and Bob had an interest there, didn't they?" I agreed. I knew that Bob had but not Fred.

Both men then got up. They said, "Tell Fred we are square now. He'll know what we mean." They then left.

When they had gone, I got a drink. It was hard to drink as I was shaking from head to foot. I phoned Fred and told him what had happened. He said, "It's your lucky day. Those guys don't normally just talk!"

Back home, Mum decided we would redecorate the living room. Jean, Willie and I made a start. We were papering when the phone rang. It was Moira, the receptionist. She told me that Fred wanted me at the Harrogate casino for an important meeting. I told Mum I had to leave. I was accused of asking Fred to ring me so I could get out of decorating. That wasn't true. It really upset me to think that she thought I would stoop so low as to do that.

At the meeting, Fred told me he had a friend who was looking for a casino manager. He said I could go if I wanted to, but if it didn't work out I could come back. I went to the Ritz Casino in Brighouse, Yorkshire, and was surprised by what I saw. The tables were old and scruffy. The croupiers weren't at all that smart in their dress; nobody seemed interested in the gaming.

I noticed that in the corner of the casino there was a boule table. This table was an offset of the original roulette table. It had four zeros instead of the normal one zero, which gave the House a better chance of making money. I didn't like it and wanted it taken away. I went to see the owner – who incidentally hadn't looked overly pleased to see me when I took the job. He told me the Boule Table (as it was known) was not to be moved, as it was his favourite table.

I then found out later that the casino had never made a profit; it was just the owner's toy. I set about changing things. Over the weeks, the losses were diminishing and I was pleased with the improvement. A couple of weeks later, the owner went abroad on holiday. I took the opportunity to move out his Boule Table. I introduced a poker night, which proved popular. For the first time we made a £1,000 profit, so I bought the staff a bottle of champagne as a reward. When the owner came back, he sacked me on the spot – I suspect because I had removed his Boule Table.

I went back to Fred, who was sorry when he heard what had happened. I went back to manage at Harrogate. I stayed at Harrogate and seemed to be doing all right. Things had more or less settled down again when Fred said there was a problem at his club in Wakefield – the manager was leaving. Fred now wanted me to take over. He asked me to go and have a look. I was to contact the manager, who would show me around. I asked, "How will I know him?"

Fred said, "Look for a scruffy, unshaven man leaning against the bar."

I went there; just as Fred had told me, he was at the bar. I introduced myself. He said (in a not-too-friendly tone), "I've heard of you and your reputation. You do things properly and you're here to take my job."

I told him, "I know you're leaving." He said that he had no choice. That surprised me. This was a cabaret club rather than just a casino. This was a lot different to what I was used to managing.

When I took over, I called a staff meeting. I did not know what the staff had been told about me. The staff seemed to accept me, with the exception of one musician. I hoped he would stay on but he refused, on the grounds that he didn't feel he could work for me. So he left.

On the first night, I spoke to the head barman. I asked him for the brewery order. He said we couldn't order unless we paid cash in advance. The alarm bells now started ringing!

I was sitting at my office desk. I tried to open a drawer. It was locked. I had to force it open. The drawer was stuffed with envelopes full of unpaid bills. I phoned Fred and told him to get here as soon as possible. The club was thousands of pounds in debt. We could not even get a bottle of milk. I looked at the books. I knew the figures had been doctored. Fred was aghast – his laid-back nature crumbling. He asked me to do my best. I made a trip to the brewery. They agreed to resume supply and we opened an account to pay on credit.

Later on in the week, I had sat down to see what artists were available for the next week's show when there was a knock at the office door. I said, "Come in. Please take a seat while I sort out next week's top of the bill."

My visitor said, "Forget it. I'm top of the bill next week."

I asked, "Who are you?"

I was told, "I am the official receiver and you have five days to pay me or the locks go on the door."

Fred found the money to pay the receiver and the show went on.

We were now coming to Christmas and all went well. After Christmas, Fred said to me, "A trawler owner named Max, who I met in Blackpool, wants to buy the Wakefield club. I would like you to assist him with any help he may need when he arrives in Wakefield. I want you to go to my other club called the Sands Casino in Blackpool to meet him." I went with Fred's girlfriend to Blackpool and she introduced me to Max.

As I mentioned earlier, my study of people told me that the man Max was a crook. He showed off his karate prowess by placing pieces of wood across the backs of two chairs then breaking the wood with his head. I was introduced to him and he said, "I'll meet you in Wakefield tomorrow." He arrived in a Mark 10 Jag accompanied by his so-called wife. He said, "I've booked a hotel and you can use the Jag. You take me to and from the hotel when I need to go there." He really was a nasty piece of work. I wasn't happy. I went to Harrogate to see Fred, who wasn't there. I sat in Fred's office to wait. I noticed a letter sticking out from a pile of unopened mail. Fred was not a tidy person. The letter was to Mr F Taylor, accounts department, so I decided to take a look. I opened the letter. It was from the bank with a returned cheque marked 'Refer to drawer'. The cheque was from Max, who was buying the club at Wakefield.

I showed Fred the letter. He said he'd sort it. I also told him I did not want to be anywhere near Max. Fred told me to stay with him for now. After I'd spent a few days with him as his lackey, Fred told me that Max was buying the Sands Casino as well as the Wakefield club. Max said that I was to get some croupiers and get them to the Sands Casino. Max told me to sack the Sands manager and all the casino staff. The croupiers I brought along to take over were ready. The manager asked me what was going on. When I told him, he panicked and phoned Fred. Fred was in a temper and said, "This is my *** club!" The croupiers I had brought, I sent home. I left the club and drove to Wakefield. I collected my things and walked out of my job. I never saw or heard from Fred again. My casino days were over. I had to go home. I was gutted.

I'd like to look back at a couple of experiences that happened to me in my early club life. I was at the posh Regency Club in Widnes. While standing at the bar, other croupiers arrived for the night's gaming. We were all sat together talking, when we could hear singing in the cabaret room. We didn't know who the singer was until we got up to look. The man singing was a very good-looking man with a lovely voice, but the songs were not the best we'd heard. I later found out the singer's name was Gerry Dorsey, a name not known to me.

When his time was up on stage, Gerry asked if he could sit with us. We agreed. While we were talking, he told us that he hoped he would get to be famous one day. We said (with a nod and a wink), "Of course you will." After Gerry left, we went to work and didn't see him. A few months later, I was watching TV at home and Gerry came on in the show. I couldn't believe what I was seeing; this man had changed his name to Engelbert Humperdinck. He was now as famous as he had hoped. I often wonder what my workmates thought, probably *Well done – he deserved it!*

Another time, I was working at the Ritz Casino at Brighouse in Yorkshire. I noticed that the weather was not good. Snow was falling. Outside, it was bitter cold. At about 2am, the weather worsened. I decided to close the casino so the staff could get home safely. When I left the club, the snow was very deep. I was worried that I might have problems getting home. I had to drive across country over the moors and very high hills. After setting off, I could hear noises in the radiator. I knew it was ice forming. I still had a very long way to go. I went through a small town called Hebden Bridge. I stopped at the police station. They gave me some hot water for the radiator. I set off again, but out in the countryside it started again. I struggled to keep going. Up the road I saw a small garage, so I pulled in. I was going to be there some time. I switched off the engine and prepared to sleep in the car. It was so cold that I could not sleep at first, but I must have dropped off eventually. I woke to hear knocking on my window. A voice said, "There's someone inside." They opened the door but I couldn't move; I was as stiff as a board. The garage staff actually carried me out of the car. They took me into the repair depot and put me in front of a large heat blower. They made me a cup of tea. I was okay.

The boss of the garage said, "If you had been there much longer, you would have been a goner." They had saved my life. I got home about 8am the following morning.

I remember when I first started my croupier career with Bob, Mum was furious. She was so mad because I often came home in the early hours. Each morning she would get up early and go round the house slamming all the doors, so I couldn't sleep. Then she would get me up, saying she had things she wanted me to do. She even told our neighbours that I was a doctor working nights at the hospital. Trouble was, all the neighbours knew what I was doing because they came to the club.

*

** A joke for your amusement **

Two pensioners were going to a house of ill repute. They walked up the garden path. The Madame was looking out of the upstairs window. She thought, *I am not wasting two of my best girls on these two. I've got two blow-up dolls in the attic. They will do.*

On the way out, one man said to the other, "How did you get on with yours?"

He said, "I don't know. She never said a word, she laid there. I thought she was dead. I gave her a cuddle and played with the bits that mattered, but when I tried to do it, nothing happened.

I could not do the business. Anyway, how did you get on?"

He said, "Much the same as you. I played with the bits at the top and just about managed to do what was necessary." I gave her a cuddle and bit her neck. The next thing that happened, she farted and flew out of the window. SHE TOOK MY TEETH WITH HER."

*

In my casino days I met quite a number of artists in various places. I said I would not name names but I have changed my mind. These people brought so much entertainment and joy, over the years, to people all over the country and abroad. I feel they should not be forgotten. Here are just a few people I have met in person...

Engelbert Humperdinck
Little and Large, Syd and Eddie
Billy Fury
Matt Monro
Danny Baker, R2-D2 *Star Wars*
Alvin Stardust, formerly Shane Fenton
Alex Higgins
Donald Peers
Max Wall
Gerry Marsden
Don Lang
Vince Hill
Tom O'Connor
Faith Brown
Colin Crompton
Karl Denver & his Trio
Bert Weedon
Helen Shapiro

... and many more appeared at our cabaret clubs and casinos. Other artists that I have just nodded to in passing, to name just a few, are ...

    The Grumbleweeds
    Scott Walker
    Mike and Bernie Winters
    Marty Wilde
    Vince Eager
    The Four Pennies
    The Searchers
    The Swinging Blue Jeans
    The Rockin' Berries

CHAPTER FOUR

Colin – Mr Belle Vue Thirties (33–42 years)

∽

Here I am back home; everything is as normal. After a few weeks, Jean told me she didn't like our lovely house in Glenview Road in Burnley as she felt uneasy. She felt like someone was watching her and often saw shadows in the house. I didn't take her very seriously, but I was finding it hard to keep up with the mortgage and decided to sell the house.

Alan by now had a job as an inspector for an insurance company. He had an office in a large empty house, owned by the company, in Ormerod Road, Burnley. With permission from his boss, it was agreed that Mum could rent the house for us all. We moved in. I did not like the place but it was somewhere to live. Jean was still at the Prestige Group, but was starting a relationship with the firm's head security man, called John. Willie was still at the same place. Mum, however, had started to learn astrology, to fit in with her spiritualism. I had no job. It wasn't going to be easy finding what I called a normal one. I wondered if I got a job how people who saw me as a croupier would react towards me. I thought they might ridicule me. The big man is no better than us. Jean told me I might get a job at Prestige but I was scared to try.

Mum was busy with her astrology. She learnt how to do readings and make charts. This was to affect all three of us. Jean was getting more serious with John. I learnt much later in life that Mum didn't like this relationship. Jean and John decided to go out for a drive but were horrified when Mum said, "I'm coming too," and got into the back seat of John's car. Mum was going to stop this romance one way or another. Mum asked Jean where John was born, his date and time of birth. Jean told her what she knew. Mum wanted to look into his chart. She told Jean that he was a nasty man and if she married him, he would beat her. Jean took it to heart and ended the relationship. Mum was chuffed and told her she was right to end it. Jean was upset but believed in what Mum had told her. She used her new-found knowledge as a weapon against us all – even telling me I wouldn't achieve anything in life. She set all of us against each other. She would talk to us. We would tell her about the things we were doing. A few days later, she would turn on us, twisting our talks with her. Telling us how rotten we were. I became the one who never told her anything. She hated me for it.

Mum was keeping us all where she wanted us, using her astronomical knowledge. Whatever we wanted to do, she had a way of stopping it. I plucked up courage and got a job at Prestige, in the machine shop. The work was heavy. The machines had heavy coils of metal that were fed into other machines. The lads helped each other. On the first day, I kept my head down, hoping no one would recognise me. One of the lads offered to help me change a big heavy coil. At lunchtime, the lads invited me to join them in a game of football. All the lads were great. They accepted me; my work worries were unfounded.

I started to go to Burnley football matches and had a season ticket for the Bob Lord Stand with Danny for one season, but I preferred the terraces. I went with Willie every Saturday and again we enjoyed our time together.

Willie never stood up for himself. Like us, he was frightened of Mum. She had this growl in her voice, which had scared us all. Mum was in control of our lives. There was no way out. Later, Mum got a little dog called Christie which was bought at Christmas – a terrier that was as bad-tempered as she was. It was one of those dogs that would let you into the house, but not out. Guess who had to take it for walkies. Willie and me, of course. In rain, hail, snow or sunshine, we had to take it out. If Mum thought we had brought it back too soon, we got it in the neck. We were told to go out again and give him a proper walk.

One day, Alan was in his office while Mum and I were alone together. When the phone rang, it was a girl I was seeing, though not seriously. We were just talking, basically passing the time, when I heard Mum making sarcastic comments in the background. She was sneering at me, saying, "You haven't said you love her. Come on, blow her a kiss."

I put the receiver down and the red mist descended. All my pent-up feelings came out and I let her have it full blast. The air was blue to purple. I finished by saying, "Get off my back and stop poking your nose into my life."

Afterwards, Alan came out and asked, "What the hell is going on?" He disappeared back into his office without waiting for an answer, obviously shocked by my language. I left the house and Mum went to bed, and she didn't get up for a couple of days – telling Jean she was too ill. I must admit to feeling guilty, although things didn't change.

A few weeks later, as I was leaving by the back gate, I heard a woman say, "Hello." It was a woman who Jean knew, called Marlene. I'd seen her a couple of times and Jean had introduced me to her. I knew she'd had a dodgy marriage that was coming to an end. She said, "It was nice to see you again," and she said that she was about to move a couple of doors away, opposite Mum's house.

As time went by, we started going out, and a few months later it got serious. When I told Mum we were going to get married, she was livid and said, "You're not seriously going to marry that trollop, are you?"

The atmosphere hit rock bottom. Even Jean said, "Don't do it." I didn't listen to either of them; I just wanted to be away from home. Mum also stipulated that I revert back to being known as Colin Nightingale because she wanted nothing to do with the marriage. I moved in with Marlene and her twelve-year-old daughter, Anne. I did go back to see Mum, hoping to clear the air but to no avail. She told me that Marlene had come to see her and was rude and threatening. I wondered at the time if that was true.

Marlene and I married, then after a couple of months Marlene had a mental breakdown – so bad she didn't know who I was. She kept saying that her ex-husband did more for her than me. I called the doctor and she was taken to hospital for special treatment. I didn't know what to do, as this was new to me. My marriage vows were for sickness and health, though I admit that I felt like running away. She was in hospital for about a month, and when she came home she wasn't quite herself yet. Alan thought the problem was that we were too near Mum. He said his company had a house in Nelson that was vacant (near Burnley, some 5 miles away). We both agreed to move, which annoyed Mum, who had not tried to help us.

I could understand why the house in Nelson was empty; it was a mess – it needed decorating or demolishing! I wasn't sure which. After six months, Marlene wasn't happy. I was at my wits' end not knowing what to do. Then Marlene came up with something that changed my life yet again. She said that she had relatives at a place called Belle Vue (in Manchester). She wanted to go and see them.

While all my troubles were piling up, Alan's marriage had collapsed and he had moved to Southend-on-Sea to take up a management position for a grocery firm. Meanwhile, it was agreed that Mum would be allowed to stay at the house and to keep the office clean for the next inspector.

Marlene and I went to Belle Vue, which I had never heard of, to find that it was a zoo as well as an amusement park. We had a meeting with one of Marlene's uncles, called Graham. Things went well, but we had no money to rent anything. Graham said he would help out with work – but to give him time. A few days later, we went back to see him. He said he could get a cheap mobile home from Blackburn and have it transported to Belle Vue.

We were ready to go, but before we went I had a long chat with Jean. This was during the time that I was dating Marlene, and hadn't seen her for about ten days. At the time, I had not thought anything of it. Mum had a habit of telling me what I was doing and where I was meeting Marlene. One day, she said, "I suppose you're meeting that woman in the café." I thought at the time, *How would she know that?*

In my talk with Jean, she told me there was a letter from Marlene, which Mum had found and opened – telling me that when Marlene came home she would meet me in the café. Mum was stealing my mail and using the contents against me. Jean begged me not to say anything to Mum. I didn't but wondered, *Is there anything that Mum won't stoop to?*

Having quit my job at Prestige, we moved to Belle Vue. My new job was to keep a check on Graham's three amusement park rides, to ensure they were safe for the public to ride on. The rides were the Ghost Train, the Caterpillar and the Octopus, all of which the fairground staff had to maintain with me. Marlene was the cashier for the Ghost Train while Anne was in school. Graham was harsh on the workers, always having to show them who was boss. He didn't want them taking advantage of him and thinking he was soft.

Graham had a daughter and two sons. His daughter looked after the home; she was eighteen and helped where she could, filling in the gaps, after his wife died. Marlene had recovered and was happy, so all was well.

I worked for Graham for about eighteen months. While I was doing some maintenance work, the park manager offered me the job of park foreman. I went to see Graham and told him of the offer. He said he would like to keep me, but if the job was better paid, I should take it. I did.

Belle Vue was owned by Trusthouse Forte. Along with the zoo, it also had a famous scenic railway. My office was on the platform by the side of the railway. In this new job, at times I worked as assistant to the park manager and got on well with everyone. I learnt how to build up the park rides, having a free hand, and sometimes had to sort out problems with the park tenants, who didn't always see eye to eye with the Belle Vue management.

I gained the respect of both sides but had one problem: I didn't drive the scenic railway train and had to put up with some nasty comments about that. I didn't drive because I was scared stiff of heights! Pete, the park engineer, took me to one side, saying, "You'll have to drive the train at some time or you'll lose the lads' respect if you don't."

Every Saturday there was speedway, and I always admired the gold speedway bike parked at the entrance. It belonged to world champion Ivan Mauger, who rode for the Belle Vue Aces team. When there was an evening race, I could watch it from the scenic railway track at night.

One night, Pete was with me and I said, "If I drive the train tonight, will you come up with me and tell me what to do?"

He said, "Most people learn in the daytime," but he came with me.

A couple of days later, I walked onto the platform. A driver was just about to set off with a train full of passengers, so I said, "I'll drive this one."

Word went round and the lads came to watch, asking, "Does he know what he's doing?" Going up was all right, but coming down the slopes was terrifying. When I stopped on the platform to let the passengers off, I received a round of applause and the lads bought me a drink, saying, "You kept that quiet." I bought Pete a drink, to thank him for his help.

The scenic railway train was one of the old-fashioned types, where you had a seat between the carriages with a brake that was used to control the train at certain parts of the track. I took the train out quite a few times and wasn't as scared as I used to be.

I got the job of foreman after the previous foreman of some forty years had passed away. I never met or even saw him, but I knew he was highly thought of. His funeral car was driven around Belle Vue, stopping at the scenic railway before going to the burial service.

A few weeks later, I went to go to the scenic railway kitchen, where the senior staff had a cup of tea before work. As I passed my office, I saw a man leaning over the desk looking out of the window. I thought it was Pete, but when I got to the kitchen there was Pete.

I said, "I thought you were in the office."

He said, "I have not been in my office since I arrived for work." He asked, "What did the man look like?" I explained what I saw. Pete said, "You've described our previous foreman. You have just seen his ghost. He was always leaning on his desk, looking out of the window. Did he have a hat on?"

I said yes, and I had said good morning to him on the way in.

A few week on, Marlene, Anne and I were about to have tea. I noticed a policeman walking towards the mobile home park. I said to Marlene, "Here comes a copper. I wonder who he is going to see. I hope no one's in trouble." To my amazement, it was me he was coming to see.

He said, "I'm looking for a Mr Nightingale."

I confirmed, "You've found him." He asked me to step outside for a moment as we needed to talk. I said, "Anything you need to say, you can say in here." He asked if I had got a parking ticket in

Colin – Mr Belle Vue Thirties (33–42 years)

Burnley a few weeks ago. I confirmed, "Yes." I had gone to Burnley to visit the family (a rare visit) then on to Burnley's home match. I thought I had parked in a good place but I got a ticket.

He said, "Okay," then left.

A few days later, he came back. He said, "I've checked your version of events, but I want to see your licence." I showed him my documents. He said, "I'd like to see your other licence." I told the policeman that when I had got my ticket I had to come back to Manchester. A couple of weeks later, I went to Burnley police station. I showed my licence to a police woman sergeant and she seemed satisfied. The copper said, "I need to check this out."

He came back yet again for a third time. He asked me to step outside the home and said, "I don't know what your game is, but I'm not going to break your arms. I just want the truth."

I told him, "I have nothing more to say. You had better arrest me." He declined to do that and went away again. When he had gone, I said to Marlene, "I think I need a solicitor."

I found one in Manchester and told her what was happening. She asked, "Is this from *Comic Cuts*?"

I said, "I wish it was."

She said, "Leave it with me."

A week later, my friend the copper reappeared. He said, "I am very sorry for the situation I put you in."

I said, "You're sorry! I live here and I'm in the public eye at Belle Vue. My neighbours are wondering who they have living near them."

He said, "We had been watching a man from the Blackley area in Manchester and had taken away his licence. He'd had some dodgy dealings. His licence had got mixed up with yours."

I asked, "Can you lot get anything right?" Thinking, *Thank goodness that's all over.*

I had been a very busy foreman one way or another. I was doing the timesheets for the staff wages and helping cash up the day's takings on many rides the firm owned. I was also doing the books, minor repairs on the scenic cars and water chute cars. We also did a water chute marathon over a period of forty-eight hours. The cars had to be moving all the time. I was part of the team, as brakeman, to slow them down in certain places. The marathon was to be monitored by the officials of the *Guinness Book of Records* (I think for 1975) and it was ratified.

I had a week off, feeling unwell, with what I thought was flu. I saw the doctor, who thought I should rest for a few days. After a few days, I felt better (though not a hundred percent). I set off to walk to my office. I felt all right. My boss pulled up in his car in front of me. He asked, "Are you all right?"

I asked, "Why?"

He said, "I have been watching you for a few minutes. You are not walking in a straight line." Apparently, I was walking round in circles – sometimes to the right and sometimes to the left. He took me back home. I flopped into the chair.

The doctor was called. I was put to bed. Marlene asked what was wrong with me. The doctor said, "I am not sure. I will come back in the morning." He said, "If he has changed colour in the morning, I will know what it is."

When I woke up next morning, Marlene told me I looked like an amber traffic light. The doctor came and said to Marlene, "He has got hepatitis. You can have it for three months before it shows itself." There was no cure; only rest.

I had two choices. One was to stay at home, but Marlene and Anne had to be careful they didn't catch it. The other was to be taken to an isolation hospital, which was recommended by the doctor. I stayed at home to rest. I felt absolutely awful, with no energy at all. The nurse came. She treated me to an enema – a wonderful experience. That night, I managed to sleep. I slept most of the morning. When I woke up, Marlene was relieved; she had thought I was dead. She had kept knocking the bed to waken me, but no luck with that. Eventually, I did wake up but only to go back to sleep. The weeks went by and I started to get better very slowly. I had been in bed for so long that I could hardly stand up.

My boss and some of the neighbours rallied round to help. My friend Harry and his daughter helped with the shopping. Harry said, "Let's try a walk and I'll come with you." He did this for a week or so, until I could walk myself. I felt a lot better. I made my way to the surgery. After I had given my name, the surgery staff came out to see me. One said, "It's the hepatitis man." I felt like royalty.

I asked the doctor, "How did I catch it?"

He said, "It's likely that you have sat on an infected toilet." We only had one very large toilet in the park, which was really dirty. As soon as it was cleaned, people messed it up again.

I was now back working, after having two months off. Starting to walk again was very difficult and it took a long time before I was fully recovered.

When we first came to Belle Vue, our mobile home was situated on a plot of land in line with other mobile homes. My next-door neighbour was a man called Harry. He lived with his daughter, Emma. I don't think they liked us at first, mainly because we were 'flatties' – a name given by travellers to people who had a different lifestyle. As time went on, we got on well and became good friends.

When I was laid up with hepatitis, Marlene had an offer of a large double-fronted stall from Pete's wife, whom she got on well with. Pete's wife was about to move to a new position on the site. Marlene asked me what I thought about it and I said, "Go for it, but I won't be able to help yet." My illness had been serious. I wasn't going to be as strong or as fit as I used to be. I couldn't do the heavy work my job required, so my work as foreman was over.

Harry kept coming to visit. I told him about the stall. He said he would help. Marlene, Anne and Harry worked hard. They put up a large 20ft board and stapled large playing cards to it. They built shelves for the prizes and were ready to open. Harry also had a double-fronted stall next to us, a rifle range, so he was there if Marlene had a problem and needed help. When she came home, Marlene tipped the takings on the table and I helped count the money.

As I started to get better, I managed to do a bit more. I felt a bit stronger each day. With my days as park foreman over, I had a lot more time on my hands. Harry came round most evenings. We would play cards; not for money, just for fun. After a time, Marlene was getting fed up with Harry coming round every night. I didn't want to upset Harry, but Marlene had a point. I suggested going to the pub to play pool. This was a good solution for both Harry and me. Marlene was happy, as she could stay at home with Anne.

Then, out of the blue, another shock. I received a call from Mum. She told me that Willie was ill and had an appointment to see a consultant at Walton Hospital in Liverpool. I had no idea that he had been unwell for a long time. Neither Mum nor Jean could be bothered to tell me. Mum didn't ask me to take him to hospital; it was more like an order. She said, "You've got the car, so you can take him." What she didn't know was that my car was off the road awaiting repair.

I told Marlene what had happened. She said, "Well, don't think you can use mine."

I said, "Please help, he's got to go to the hospital."

She was adamant, adding, "I don't like your mum one bit and you don't jump when she says you should." Mum hadn't given me much notice; he had to be at the hospital in two days. It meant I had to travel from Manchester to Burnley, then to Liverpool to find Walton Hospital in one day. Again, I pleaded with Marlene for her car. Again, it was, "No." We had a real domestic, but I found her keys and drove off in her car.

I got Willie to the hospital, but on the way I could see how ill he was. All Mum would say was that he would have to have an operation on his left leg. He saw a consultant and after he had examined him, I asked, "When is his next appointment?" Wondering how many visits I would have to make.

The consultant said, "There won't be any more." I was stunned when he said that, and he followed by saying, "I am sorry." I was not sure what to make of that.

After getting back to Burnley, I told Mum what had happened. She said, "I am not surprised, but thanks for taking him." By this time, it was dark outside – about 9.30pm. On the way back home, about 10 miles out of Manchester, steam started coming out from under the bonnet. I stopped. I waited until the engine had cooled then lifted the bonnet to find the fan belt missing. I drove a bit further until the steam started again. I stopped until it cooled down again. It took until 10.30pm to get home.

When I got in, a row started. I told Marlene the fan belt was broken. The air became blue. I said, I had only taken her car in an emergency. That didn't help! A couple of weeks later, Mum told me on the phone that Willie was in hospital and not likely to survive. He died later. When I went home, the atmosphere was icy and didn't look like getting any better.

It was getting near Christmas. Every year, the circus was held in King's Hall. Children's rides were erected in King's Hall Square, which was between the hall entrance and the amusement park stalls. A new ride was given to us to be put up. The management wanted it up and running straight away. There weren't any instructions with it, but as we had built these rides up plenty of times, we didn't see a problem. There was! No matter what we did, it didn't seem to fit together. We kept having a platform section left over. I went to see the management. They didn't have a clue either. We decided to admit defeat. The electrician turned up, asking, "Where is this ride I'm supposed to wire up?"

I said, "You can wire it up but we don't know how to put it up."

He started laughing and I asked, "What's funny?"

He replied, "You lot. I take it you haven't seen one of these before, but I have. It's American and you put it together the opposite way to a British one, and the wiring's the same." We were all red-faced. In the end, we put it up together, wired it up and it was ready to go.

Everything was going well when I heard there was a small stall that was to become available. I managed to get it for a very silly rent. It was on the end of our parade. We now had our dart stall, Harry's rifles, a Hall of Mirrors and our new stall – all in a line. We decided to put in American donuts. Harry helped us set it up. I bought an industrial mixer for the donut mix and prepared to open up. While we were setting up, we noticed that King's Hall was being altered, after the circus, for a band called T. Rex, who had arrived for a rehearsal before their show. As Marlene and I were working, we spotted a man running around the rides. This man kept running around the rides, one way then the other. I said hello to him. He did not reply; he just smiled and kept running.

Marlene said, "That's Marc Bolan." I thought, *Wow!* We never saw him again. We didn't go to his concert; it was for one night only. A few weeks later, we heard of his unfortunate death in a car crash. We thought what a waste of a life, as well as an iconic artist.

The donut stall was a roaring trade. I didn't know that donuts were so popular. We were going through the donut mix for fun. I was ordering twenty large bags at a time and we were making money. On the Queen's Silver Jubilee, the park was packed and I had a queue, probably 50 yards long.

Harry came to me and said, "What are you doing? Look at your queue! If people have to queue like that, you are losing money."

I asked him, "What should I do?"

To which he answered, "Double your price." I was reluctant but he insisted. "Just do it."

I did double the price and the queue was still there. We had started at 9am and finished at 11pm. It took ages to count the takings! The only downside to having this stall was being next to the Hall of Mirrors. They played George Formby songs all day, every single day of the season. It drove me mad. I was losing the will to live, and only our takings kept me sane.

We were nearing the end of the season (in 1980). Rumours were flying around that Belle Vue was to be sold. Marlene and I discussed how this would affect us. She suggested I find a job, which I knew would not be easy. She said she didn't want to look for work. This created an atmosphere. A few days later, she told me that she had phoned some relatives in Mablethorpe, Lincolnshire, who had said she would be welcome. We had both visited them before for a few days, but they didn't seem to accept me. It seemed that this invitation was for her only.

I agreed that Marlene could keep the mobile home and run the two stalls until Belle Vue was closed. This would give her some income to live on then pay to transport the mobile home to Mablethorpe. We agreed to part. This happened so quickly that I was in a daze. We went from getting on so well and making a good living to having absolutely nothing. When Belle Vue closed, my work was over and our relationship was finished. How could this happen? The following morning, I packed a suitcase of clothes, called a taxi and went to Manchester Piccadilly Station to buy a one-way ticket to Euston.

Once again, my world had collapsed. What would I do next? My life was like a ROLLERCOASTER, climbing uphill then crashing back down.

On the journey down south, my mind went back again to my Belle Vue days. I remembered I was asked to assist a film crew that was making the film *Stardust*. It starred Adam Faith and David Essex. My job as park foreman was to make sure as many of the rides and stalls as possible were open, including all lights at Belle Vue being on.

Some of the showmen who owned the rides were happy to comply, because their equipment would be seen in the film. A couple of the showmen who refused to assist wanted paying. I could understand why, as their staff could be working all night with the lights burning. In the end, there was no agreement. The film company worked around it. The film was shot in winter; it was very cold. In fact, there was a light snowfall.

A mobile camera was used for some shots. A couple of the film crew and myself had to push it around between the rides and stalls. We even had to sit on it to balance it on uneven ground. Filming went on until the early hours, with occasional breaks. It was a great experience. In King's Hall, they were also filming the Scary Cats Concert, but I didn't get the time to go and watch. It was a really good night, with a good payday for me. When the filming was finished, I still had to close the amusement park. I thanked all those who helped make the film the success it was. Then it was back to normal the next day.

The film was shot in 1974, when I was a mere thirty-six-year-old. I was forty-two when I left Belle Vue in 1980. Yet I still had memories of all the other concerts, including the Bay City Rollers, the Osmonds and the International Pop Proms.

I was told to go to King's Hall to assist other staff for the Bay City Rollers concert. All the gates to the park were closed and the security staff were in place. It was to be a huge concert. The crowd who had tickets were allowed in the park. At the gates, young girls were trying to climb over. The security staff found that they were stretched. Belle Vue was such a large place that it was difficult to stop some girls getting in. Most were caught and thrown out, but some were offering sex if we let them in. They were ejected, as far as I know. There were at least a thousand people in the square in front of the hall, all impatient to get in. They started to bang on the glass doors, trying to force the doors open. The door staff, including myself, were told to stand at least 20 feet away from the doors (which were beginning to bend), in case the doors broke and the crowd stampeded in. We held out. The girls were baying, "We want the Rollers." The sound was deafening. Eventually, we did manage to get them all in, without too much trouble. The concert went very well. The band played all their favourite hits, which pleased the crowd. It was hard to hear the music for the screaming of the girls. Some passed out through mass hysteria. The medical room was very busy, as were we, ferrying girls who had fainted to the medics. After the show, the security men moved the fans away from the hall's exits and out of the park. It was a very difficult night for the staff, but a night to remember, seeing the Rollers up close. We were glad when it was over.

A few weeks after the Bay City Rollers, we were told that the Osmonds were due to appear at the Hall in a few weeks. We thought, *Here we go again*. The security men were much the same. We still had problems stopping the fans climbing over the gates. Some girls were pretending to faint so we would bring them in for medical attention, hoping they could hide somewhere and get in. We made sure that didn't work. There were again hundreds of people outside in the square, very noisy but generally patient, not like the Rollers fans. When the crowds were in the concert, you couldn't hear anything with the screaming. It settled down as the show progressed and you could then hear the music. On stage with the Osmonds were four Japanese karate experts. They had their own security guards around the stage. My position, along with others, was to stand on the edges of the stage to stop the girls reaching the Osmonds. I would say it was a great honour to be able to say I was on stage with the Osmonds. I had to carry a girl who had fainted to the medical room. The room was packed with girls who had passed out, much the same as with the Rollers. The show was great, with Donny and Marie singing their number 1 hits. The show went well over time but nobody complained. Everyone was enjoying themselves. After the show finished, all the staff were exhausted.

I went to many concerts of the acts of the day. The first was Elton John. I was told by King's Hall staff that Elton only wanted paying fans to be allowed in, no Belle Vue staff or management. I did manage to slip in. I was told that his own personnel were walking down the aisles, counting the fans sitting down. Apparently, the ticket money had to match the fans in the hall, before the show started. I really enjoyed the show. I also got to see the James Last Orchestra and Don Williams. I did see others but at my age remembering them all is difficult. I saw about half an hour of Demis Roussos, but I had to leave early for work reasons. Before I went in, I noticed that the cars parked near the Hall were mostly Rolls-Royce, Mercedes, BMW and Jaguars, no rubbish. As the occupants went into the Hall, there was a vicar standing by the door with a large bucket. People were putting large amounts of paper cash into the bucket. After a while, he would leave his post and disappear. He would then return and collect more money. I asked one of my staff to follow him. The vicar would go to his car, lift the boot and tip the money in and return. I don't know to this day whether he was a vicar or some lucky man making a fortune. I got an invite to a special event: the International Pop Proms. It featured stars from the fifties and sixties. It was a brilliant night. I felt very sorry for one singer, American Guy Mitchell. He was a special guest at the Proms, long after his famous days had come to an end. He came on stage and sang a couple of his hits, but would then not leave the stage. His manager and the compère tried hard to get him to leave. He may have been unwell, because he was unsteady on his feet. They eventually eased him from the stage. It was sad to see him like that. In his day, he was a true singing icon.

*

** Another amusing joke **

A man in a smart suit with a very posh car was walking round a building site talking to the men. He was spotted by the foreman, who shouted, "What are you doing? Don't you know this is a private building site?"

The man said, "I was just asking the men if there was any work going."

The foreman said, "With that car and your posh suit, you're no builder."

The man said, "Okay. You're right. Actually, I am a professional gambler and you look like a man who likes a gamble. Do you fancy a bet?"

The foreman said, "What sort of bet?"

The gambler said, "All right, I bet you £50 that by five o'clock, you will have a rupture."

The foreman said, "It's a bet, but I'm going to sit in my office and not move until five o'clock."

The gambler said, "Okay. I'll see you at five."

When he came back, he said to the foreman, "How are you?"

He said, "I'm fine. You've lost your bet."

The gambler said, "I want to see for myself, so drop your trousers." The foreman did as he was told. The gambler said, "You look okay." Then he picked up a trowel and placed it between the foreman's legs. He lifted up the foreman's manhood and said, "No rupture!"

The foreman said, "Give me the money, you have lost."

The gambler said, "I have only lost part of the bet, but I have won plenty. When you saw me on the site earlier talking to the men, I worked out there were about fifty men. I bet them all £10 that I would have the foreman's balls on a trowel by five o'clock. I've had a good day. Good afternoon."

CHAPTER FIVE

Colin – Mr Try Anything Forties (43–50 years)

∾

After my reminiscing, it is back to reality. On arrival at Euston, I took the tube to Liverpool Street, a train to Southend-on-Sea and a bus to Rochford, near Southend Airport. I eventually arrived at my brother's house.

As you can imagine, Alan being surprised to see me was the understatement of the year. I dare say I could have gone back to Burnley, but I know Mum would have had a field day. I would have had to put up with her snide remarks, day in, day out. Jean would have been pleased to see me.

I settled in quite well with Alan, though over the years he had been going away a lot, so I didn't know him that well. We were different types of brothers. While I was completely outgoing, he was the opposite. I could talk to him easily but he would not know what to say back. He did love cooking. He made some lovely dinners and puddings, which I enjoyed. He cooked and I washed up. I knew I needed to find work. I got a job with a cleaning firm. It did not last long, as I was almost electrocuted using one of their machines which was faulty.

I again had to find work. I took a walk round an industrial estate nearby. I spotted a notice on a factory door which read 'Part-time toilet cleaner wanted'. I thought what a come-down after what I had done before. I asked to see the manager and applied. I got the job and was due to start the following day.

The manager said I had to meet the boss before I started. He wanted to know a bit about me. We chatted for about half an hour. He said, "How do you feel about being assistant storeman, instead of being a toilet cleaner? We will teach you how to drive a forklift truck and other aspects of the job."

Needless to say, I jumped at the opportunity. I said, "Yes and thank you."

The forklift I found easy. While driving around the yard, I tidied up each area. I was really happy, getting on well with the men and my job going well. It was a commercial body building firm, making bodies for lorries. When panels of steel were needed, I would get them. I loved the job. I was also able to drive the firm's van up to London for parts. It was not long before disaster hit again; I was made redundant. The men went to the boss saying, "Don't let him go, he's needed." Yet I had to go, and was knocked down again.

A few days before I was due to leave, one of the men told me a job was available at a builders' merchants round the corner. He had put in a good word for me with the boss. I went for an interview and got the job. I didn't feel that comfortable about the position for some reason; perhaps it was my very good sixth sense. While walking round the office, I went through a door. On the other side someone had left a bucket, which I managed to trip over. I said, "What's that doing there?"

A voice said, "Why don't you look where you're going?" I got a dirty look.

I started the following Monday as a salesman. The person I met was the transport manager. Guess what. You're right. It was the man with the bucket. He made it plain that he didn't like me. My name was mud with other staff members. I put up with it for some months, until the boss called him in. He told him to leave me alone. Fat chance! Word got round that I had spent time in the north of England. I had never told anyone about my other jobs. It could be some of the northern terms that gave me away. I didn't like the firm one bit. Then it got worse.

The boss' brother replaced the transport manager. He was just as bad. One day, the boss called me to his office. He asked, "Would you like an office job upstairs? The job entails doing the company's banking." He said, "You can use my Mercedes to go to the bank." Things seemed to be looking up. But, no! My job meant working closely with his brother. It didn't work. He took every chance to cause me problems. I was wondering how long this job would last.

I shared an office with three other people – two men and a woman. One day, I was with the men. We were talking football. I let it out that I followed Liverpool. The woman told me she was a West Ham supporter and didn't like Liverpool. I said, "It's only a game." She was never nice to me again. She wouldn't even say good morning. I wondered, *What's wrong with this place?*

I had moved upstairs but still had contact with some of the customers. A man who used to come in for gas bottles, for his plant hire firm, said to me that his boss was looking for a manager for his plant hire shop in Southend. Did I fancy it? I said, "I don't know anything about plant hire," so I wasn't sure.

A few days later, he said that his boss was willing to talk to me, so I went to see him and he was with his business partner. One was laid-back, the other quite abrupt, which unnerved me. He said, "I will show you what to do." I thought it couldn't be as bad as where I was now. It was more money. I had the use of a firm's truck. When I was on holiday, he would lend me a car and fill it up with petrol.

His ex-wife lived above the shop. She could be a little volatile, but he said, "If it gets awkward, just tell me."

I went back to the builders' merchants. I said, "I've got some great news for you. I'm leaving. I'm sure you will find someone else to bully." The boss never said a word.

I started my new job. I found that my boss' bark was worse than his bite. I met his ex-wife; she was completely neurotic. She could fly off the handle at a moment's notice. I went in early one morning to sort out equipment for a delivery. This was not a quiet job at the best of times. She came downstairs shouting, "What time do you call this?" She stormed off. Five minutes later, she came down, full of apologies, saying, "I misread the time." After a while, we found a happy medium. We got on a little bit better. She still had the odd moments but nothing a cup of tea wouldn't solve.

On one occasion, two men wanted me to deliver some equipment for them to the cinema in town. The job had to be done in two days. They needed the goods delivered at 6am. I said, "I don't start 'till 7.30am." Though, in the end, I agreed. "Okay, but it's a one-off." They paid the deposit then did the job. They phoned to ask me to pick the equipment up. I got the goods back but there no sign of the men. Three weeks went by. I phoned and left messages but got no answer. I went to the cinema and spoke to the manager. He said, "I have never spoken to the men."

I then asked, "Are you going to pay me?"

He said, "No, the men have a contract with Odeon Cinemas."

He did give a contact phone number. I went back to the shop. I rang the number. A voice growled, "What do you want?"

I told him, "I don't like being messed about." I explained what had happened.

He yelled, "How much do they owe?" He slammed the phone down. A week later, I got a cheque from Odeon Cinemas for the full amount, with an apology. The men came in a couple of days later and said they were sorry; they had lost the contract. I said, "You only have yourselves to blame; not me." So they left.

Life was on the up. Everything was going well living with Alan. His job as manager at the grocer's seemed safe and I was in work. When I had a holiday, true to his word, the boss supplied a car with a full tank of petrol.

I visited Mum and Jean. Mum never asked what had happened with Marlene. Nothing much had changed; I still had to pick up Jean from work, yet there was an atmosphere – it felt that something was about to erupt, so I got ready to leave. Jean was upset; she told me she couldn't do anything right. If she said the wrong thing, Mum would go to bed for a few days saying she had colic.

Jean was still working but Mum would phone her at work. She would ask her to come home because she felt ill. When Jean arrived home, she said she felt better. This happened many times, yet Jean said her boss was very understanding. When Mum went to bed, Jean had to wash and dry her. She would say she was a rotten nurse. Jean begged me not to say or do anything because Mum would take it out on her. When I got back to Southend, I told Alan, but he didn't say anything – it didn't seem to bother him.

I went back to work after my holiday. I was serving a customer, when a man who I later found out was called Simon and a very good-looking blonde girl called Judith walked in. I had seen him before but not her. He said, "I don't want to hire anything. My partner, Giles, and I have a building firm in London. We are going to open a plant hire shop. I've been here before and I like the way you always seem to be cheerful. I wondered if you would consider managing our shop."

I was shocked, I replied, "I don't know."

He said, "If you are not doing anything on Sunday, I'll pick you up early. Come to London and I'll show you our shop." If you like what you see, I'll give you more than you're being paid here."

I went. I wasn't sure it was situated in a good place, but I wasn't happy in Southend.

I had done my best to keep in work, no matter what the circumstances. At weekends, I would wander around town, thinking about the good times in the past. I used to go into the department stores. I would look in the mirrors, thinking, *Who would want you?* I had hit an all-time low. I said yes to Simon. I would go to London and take my chance. They offered to find me a flat. Simon's partner, Giles, had a few houses in the area and the rents were reasonable. He would also pay me £35 a week extra London allowance. I told Alan what had happened and he said, "Go for it and good luck."

It was now 1984. I was ready to go, when I suddenly fell ill with a serious chest infection, laryngitis and pharyngitis. I was laid up for nearly two months. Simon said, "Don't worry, the shop's not ready to open. Get yourself better and come when you are fit."

After my illness, I was ready to go. London, here I come! I was looking forward to a new start and challenge all over again.

As I said earlier, the new shop was not situated in a good place. It was on a T-junction, where parking was not ideal for loading purposes, for local vans or cars. Here I was, trying to do my best. I now found that the promised flat was unavailable. It had to be re-let because of my illness. I had to commute from Southend to London and back each day (not helpful) until another flat became available.

The journey from Southend was difficult. I had to leave home at 5.30am, travel up the A13 to join the Rochester Way before 6.30am. If I was any later, I would catch commuter traffic, which created a delay of up to two hours on one section and another one and a half hours in Lewisham. On return, I would have to leave work at 4.30pm. With hold-ups at Catford and the Dartford Tunnel, I wouldn't get home until 8pm. Thankfully, Alan had a meal ready for me when I got in. Once, I got up in the morning to find about 3 foot of snow on the ground – completely covering the car. Work was out of the question. Nobody else could travel, so it did not matter that I could not get there.

I got my promised flat in 1985 and moved to Peckham Rye, not far from the shop. The shop still wasn't ready to open because Simon was still running his building firm from it. I was helping some of his labourers clean it up. All the new hire equipment was coming in. We all rallied round to sort things out.

There was a time when I wondered what I was doing there. The shop was nowhere near opening and Simon didn't seem overly bothered. I had a word with him because I was bored to tears. Simon decided to cover the windows all around the shop with a product called Windolene. No one could see in or out.

We could see the local people trying to peer into the shop to find out what it was going to be. As I was going out, a woman stopped me and asked me what the shop would sell. With a deadpan face, I said, "It's a high-class sex shop." Word went round the town like wildfire. At least Simon saw the funny side. The locals were not impressed. After a short while, we told them the real trade of the premises and the unrest then died down.

My new flat in Peckham Rye was absolutely beautiful. It was in a large house divided into flats. I shared the house with five other people, all of whom were city slickers. I felt a bit out of place. I knew the other tenants were wary of me because I worked for Giles. He had a habit of telling me to turn off the heating if it was on after a certain hour. I did it only now and again, as I wanted to keep on the right side of my new housemates.

The men in the house were friendly, as they understood that I was in a difficult position. Two of the women looked down their noses at me. I didn't care because there was no need to talk to them. I did have a bit of a problem in the mornings, having to get up early for work. Someone was always in the bathroom when I got there. It was annoying. I had no idea who it was. Naturally, I assumed it was one of the girls because they were in the bathroom for a long time. I tried for a few days to get in without success. I got up very early in an effort to beat the other person to the bathroom. It worked. I got in first. I could hear someone trying the door handle. *Hard luck,* I thought. When I came out, there was a woman waiting. She had an expression that said everything. I don't think she was happy. She was not one of the snooty girls. Her name (I found out later) was Gillian, a private school teacher who needed to get up early to travel to her school. When we did speak, it was cordial. We seemed to get on well. I knew she was not too keen on the other girls because she was more intelligent. I also got on with another man called Brandon, from New Zealand. He was a really nice man who loved sports. He got the other men together and we went across the road and played cricket in the park. The cricket games became a regular event on summer evenings.

One day, I was boiling some eggs for dinner. While they were boiling, I went to my room for something. On the way back to the kitchen, I met Brandon on the stairs. He said, "I am on my way to town for a game of pool. Do you fancy a game?"

I said "Yes". He suggested playing for £25 a frame. That seemed a lot, but as I'd played for the Belle Vue team a few years back, I thought, *Why not?*

We were to play four games over a couple of days. I eventually won all of them. After the first two games, which took about an hour, we went back to the flat. Brandon went upstairs. I noticed a smell of burning from the kitchen. I had completely forgotten my eggs! There was the pan with a big hole in it. The eggs had exploded all over the place. There was egg stuck to the cupboards, on the windows; everywhere you looked, there was egg. I was horrified. This was going to take me hours of cleaning. I was swearing under my breath, when I heard a voice behind me. "What have you done?" I meekly explained that I had been out with Brandon and completely forgotten the eggs. I started looking for cloths. Gillian said, "You do the windows and I'll do the cupboards." I couldn't have been more grateful for her help. When we had cleaned up, we sat and talked for ages. We became good friends afterwards. The house was back to normal. Thankfully, no one else came home. The smell finally went; everything was back to normal.

The house had communal areas which were open-plan and

decorated to a high standard. It was Giles' pride and joy. The bathroom was fantastic, with a three-quarter sunken bath. The staircase lights were on a timer. Decent parking outside, which was a real bonus in London. It was like a palace – without the enhancement of egg decoration.

At the shop, Simon had moved out with his labourers. They all came to the shop early in the morning to discuss the day's work before leaving. I stayed at the shop with Simon's girlfriend, whom I mentioned earlier. She was called Judith, a very pretty girl, thin as a post. Customers thought she was my daughter. She lived in Southend with Simon. She came up to sort out the finances. We got on really well, which helped. I learnt a lot about doing the books. I had done some books at the hire shop in Southend. I set about doing the books, VAT, wages and tax. Giles was pleased that I was able to do that. Initially, I found it hard. I had to refer back to the previous week's entries. Over the next few weeks, I found I could do the books easily.

Simon knew I was going to Southend to see Alan, who had moved to Westcliff-on-Sea after his boss had offered him a large flat over the grocery shop he was managing. Simon asked if I would do him a favour and take Judith home to Southend. He had a look on his face that said, *Don't ask questions.* When we got in my car, I could see she had been crying. I didn't ask what was wrong until she said Simon had dumped her. We made small talk for the rest of the journey. When I got her home, she said, "Thank you, you never know, we might have a drink sometime," but I never saw her again.

Gillian and I became what people today call an item. We would have dinner most weekends. We would spend most of our free time together. Gillian's mum and dad had come from Woking in Surrey where she had lived. They wanted to meet me. I think her dad wanted to check me out, to see if I was right for his daughter. Her mum seemed to like me, but I think her dad was hedging his bets. He seemed worried about the age gap of seventeen years. Eventually, everything worked out well.

Gillian mentioned that she was going on holiday to Cornwall with her parents and asked if I would like to go. I said "Yes" and it was all agreed. I told Giles that I wanted to take a week's holiday. He said,

"No, there is no one to cover the shop." He was adamant that I couldn't take the time off. I had to tell Gillian that I couldn't go and she had to tell her folks.

Our relationship almost came to a sudden end. She did forgive me (eventually) after I got the look and a few unwelcome words. My apologies fell on deaf ears. This problem would not have happened when Judith was at the shop; it would have been easy for her to have taken over.

It wasn't long after that Gillian left the Peckham Rye house. She had been offered a new job nearer home. We agreed to keep in touch; she would come and see me at weekends when she could. Back at the shop, trade was mediocre and there was nothing I could do to improve it. We had various ideas but nothing positive. Giles suggested I move to a flat above the shop.

The house was similar to the one at Peckham, with five new flatmates to get to know. Both the men and the women were very nice – no airs and graces. It was a very relaxed place; all the tenants were a cheery lot. I played football with two of the lads. One was called Roli; his full name was hard if not impossible to pronounce. We called him Roli for short. Giles didn't like Roli; he knew all about tenants' rights. He wouldn't look for work but about a year after, Roli left the house and the next time I saw him, he was a newsreader for BBC1. That was a real surprise.

At Peckham, I packed up my things and moved to my new home in Forest Hill, about a mile away. I look back at my time at Peckham: the city slickers, Brandon and the egg fiasco. I didn't mention one of the male city slickers, a man called Nick. He said he followed boxing closely. We both knew the middleweight champion of the world was Marvelous Marvin Hagler. He was due to fight the retired former champ, Sugar Ray Leonard, who came out of retirement just for this fight. Nick told me that he had put his whole month's wages on Hagler to win, as Sugar Ray hadn't fought for ages. I do read about sport a lot and I told Nick I had read that Sugar Ray had had three fights with others behind closed doors, and I bet him 10 pence that Sugar Ray would win. The following day, Nick was in tears; Sugar Ray had flattened Hagler. He was crying, "I can't pay my rent or buy food." I thought he had followed boxing closely. If he had, he would have known about Sugar Ray before betting all that money. I never got my 10 pence!

I had settled in well at the Forest Hill house. The area was not as nice as Peckham and the house was not as posh, but it was more me. Gillian visited most weekends and we cooked some nice meals. I had also made friends with a couple of lads and we went to the snooker hall quite a bit. Their names were Ray and James.

Ray was a roofer and James was self-employed. Ray was quite laid-back, but James was a cheeky, crazy type of chap. He also had a large house, which he was renovating. It had a tenant, who had a room upstairs, and she kept overfilling the bath, and the water came through the ceiling and out of the light fittings. She did this a few times, saying she had forgotten the taps were on. He never seemed to get annoyed. I went there with Ray and a couple of other lads to play pool; we had some good nights. James and Ray were motorbike enthusiasts and they told me they were going abroad on a motorbiking holiday. They would be away for a week or so. I didn't know they had a boat moored in Ibiza. They thought they would give it a run out, as they had decided to sell it.

They arrived in Ibiza and took the boat out. While out at sea, they got caught up in one of Ibiza's vicious storms. Ray was at the wheel when a heavy wave hit the boat and tossed him into the sea. He drowned. James fired a distress rocket, as the boat was in trouble, and tied himself to the mast. His distress flare was picked up by a Greenpeace vessel, which came alongside. James could not undo the rope tying him to the mast. As the large vessel was lifted up by the waves, James' boat was sucked under the vessel, which crushed it. Both of my friends died at sea that day. Their bodies were never found. A very sad time for all that knew them.

I was laid in bed one morning in 1987. I woke up about 6.30am to a rumbling noise from the roof. It seemed to go on for some while. I got up and looked out of the window to see roof tiles raining down from the roof. Looking across the road, there were large oak trees bending in half and some trees had fallen across the road. The wind was hitting my window so hard; I had never seen anything like this before. I got dressed before checking whether our shop below was safe.

Colin – Mr Try Anything Forties (43–50 years)

I later learnt that this was the London hurricane. We fortunately had no damage to the shop but the traffic, what little was around, was brought to a standstill. I rang Gillian to see if she was okay. Thankfully, she was, as it was mostly woodland and countryside around Woking that had taken the brunt. Even Sevenoaks had become ONE OAK. In Peckham, there were large holes in the pavements where large oak trees had once stood. The roots had completely torn the paving apart. It was a couple of weeks before Gillian was able to come and see me.

On one Saturday I wanted to see Liverpool play at Hillsborough in the FA Cup. We sat down to watch the game on TV. Just as it was about to start, there was panic on the terraces. We did not know what was happening. It was an horrific sight. We could see fans trying to get from the stands to the upper tiers, also fans trying to get onto the pitch. We did not know what was happening. It was obvious that the match could not start. We then saw ambulances driving onto the pitch, and stewards using the advertising hoarding to carry people who were injured. The match was finally abandoned as there was a major incident unfolding. Only later did we learn that fans had been allowed into an already full area, causing them to be crushed together with no escape route. The incident caused the deaths of many fans. It wouldn't be until many days later on before we knew the full extent of the death toll. Being a long-time fan, I watched with a lump in my throat. What followed was many years of inquiries into what had happened and who was responsible. It would take thirty years before the inquiry found that the fans were wrongly accused of causing the disaster.

Another sad event happened a couple of days later. Gillian phoned me in the evening to say that her grandma had passed away. Gillian had visited her grandma in Southampton during that day and she had appeared to be well, but when Gillian got home she received a phone call. It was from her grandma's neighbour who had gone to check on her as usual. She was sat in her normal chair and must have fallen asleep and died almost immediately after Gillian had left. Obviously, this was a big shock. I got in the firm's van and drove to Woking to comfort Gillian in her distress and stayed a couple of hours before driving back home. Later, there was the funeral, and after that the house had to be cleared ready for sale. Gillian would have most of the furniture.

We decided to go down to Southampton to collect the furniture from Grandma's house. I left London and went to Woking to collect Gillian; we drove to Southampton. We loaded the van with the furniture, drove back to Woking for a cup of tea, then on to London. After a break, we set off to Southend to unload the furniture at Alan's house and had some lunch. Alan had previously agreed to store the furniture until it was needed. We then spent the night at Alan's before setting off to London and on to Woking to drop Gillian off. Having done all that, I went back to London then back to work on Monday for a rest!

At the shop, Giles and I had a meeting. The shop takings had improved a little but not enough for Giles' liking. In an effort to build things up, Giles agreed to make me a non-executive director, so I had more authority to negotiate with customers and business contacts. We agreed to try this for a few months in the hope of boosting trade. Simon and Giles had parted company, as Simon wanted to spend more time with his building firm.

Simon asked me to go for a drink with himself and a friend. I didn't drink but he talked me into having one glass of whisky. I hadn't noticed that he had got me a treble. After being with them for about an hour and a half, I was three sheets to the wind. They helped me back to the house, but I couldn't get the key in the lock. So Simon unlocked the door and helped me get inside and yelled good night. Somehow, I got upstairs without anyone noticing and I went to my bedroom. My head was spinning, along with the room. I kept waiting for the bed to come round near enough for me to get on it. I finally fell onto it and went to sleep. I had a thick head in the morning. On my arrival at the shop, a man with a lorry wanted twenty-four long scaffold boards. It was not funny. I had broken my own rules. After leaving my casino life, I had told everyone I would never ever set foot in a casino again or have a drink.

Giles came to see me and said he was going to sell the shop. He said our new arrangement was not working. Despite all our best efforts, he thought it was time to move on but wanted me to handle the sale.

Colin – Mr Try Anything Forties (43–50 years)

Gillian and I often went to Alan's at the weekend and on one occasion I had mentioned being concerned about the future of the shop and what that would mean for me. Another conversation was, could we start a business of our own? If so, where? I suggested we went back to Burnley (Lancashire) to see what was available. Alan said, "It's worth trying."

I was still living at the house and knew that a sister of one of my customers was involved with mortgages. He said, "She would be able to help if needed." I decided this was the direction to try.

I asked Gillian, "If I go to Burnley, how do you feel about coming with me?"

That's when she hit me with a bombshell! She said, "I'll come, but not as a single woman."

I wasn't expecting that! I had to consider what she said and think about it very seriously – for some sixty seconds! – before asking, "Do you really mean it?"

She said, "Yes", and I said, "Yes". Problem solved.

We left Alan's and after I had taken Gillian home to Woking, I went back to London. Back at the shop, Giles said, "It looks like I've got a sale." He asked me to meet the buyers and do a stocktake. After that, the sale went through smoothly.

I thought, *Here we go again!* I wasn't too down about it. I had known on coming to the shop that I wasn't happy where the shop was situated. I felt it was partly my fault; I wasn't experienced with the London scene and didn't know anyone. After the sale, I took some time off and Giles lent me his car, so I drove to Burnley and told Mum and Jean I was coming back up north.

Jean was pleased, but Mum was not. She asked, "Why do you want to come back here? People know you and where you worked, and people don't forget." I thought they would have done after thirty years.

Having promised Gillian I would phone her when I got to Burnley, I asked Mum, "Could I use the telephone?"

She said bluntly, "No – I suppose you've got some floozy to ring. If you want to phone, go out and find a phone box."

I did eventually and I told Gillian, "Things haven't changed, and when you meet her, watch out."

While I was in Burnley, I bought all the local papers and put them in the car boot. I left as soon as I could. You may wonder why I went back. It was because property was very cheap and we couldn't afford London prices. Gillian's mum and dad (Eileen and Bill) invited me to live in Woking with them, as I was about to marry their daughter. I thanked them. I said goodbye to Giles and the shop and moved in at Gillian's, knowing her folks wanted to get to know me better, which was to be expected.

One of the things I missed in London was watching Concorde flying over the shop. It was quite spectacular seeing it bank at an angle to get on the flight path to land at Heathrow Airport. You could hear Concorde coming miles before you saw it. The noise was unbelievable. It came over the shop at 6pm on the dot. You could set your watch by it.

Gillian and I drove to Burnley at the weekend, found a B&B and spent the weekend looking at various shops that were for sale. We decided to look at corner shops that were suitable, as we both had retail experience. We eventually picked one in a place called Colne – a few miles from Burnley – which looked a good prospect. As time passed, we went through the sales procedure and completed the sale.

CHAPTER SIX

Colin – Mr C&G Fifties (50–60 years)

∾

We went back to Woking to arrange for removals. We had a bit of a rush to organise packing and say our goodbyes to friends before we were ready to go. We loaded my van with personal items. We said goodbye to Gillian's parents and set off for Burnley. We stayed the night at the B&B and took over our shop the following afternoon.

On our way to the shop, we stopped at Mum and Jean's house and I introduced Gillian to them. Jean welcomed Gillian and Mum provided tea and cakes. All seemed well; but not for long. When I was alone with Mum, she said, "You won't get rid of her, and I don't like the way she brushed the crumbs of my cake onto the floor."

I said, "Gillian has been brought up better than to do that." We left for the shop.

At the shop, the previous owner Mrs Jones and I did the stocktake. We paid for the stock. Mrs Jones then threw the keys onto the table and left quite quickly. At that time, I wondered why she had gone so quickly. We started to sort out the things from the van. The removal lorry arrived from Woking with three removal men. Gillian directed the removal men to put things in the necessary rooms. All the boxes were marked. We had to get the house organised. We only had a couple of days before opening the shop. It was a frantic couple of days. Mrs Jones did not give us a list of suppliers. Only the milkman called to welcome us.

We opened up in August 1989. Our new shop was named C and G Stores. We seemed to get on with the local people. There was an engineering factory across the road that opened an account with us for tea, coffee and other goods. We opened six days a week, from

8am to 7pm. We were open early enough to catch the schoolkids on their way to school. They would come back at lunchtime, as did the factory workers, who wanted hot pies and sandwiches. Some of the kids also came after school, and trade was busy.

The shop was close to the town centre; it was not large. There was a lot of housing around us, but we were also near to open country with a view of the famous Pendle Hill, the home of the often-written-about Pendle witches. On Sundays, we drove around the Colne area and visited countryside restaurants, taking in the breathtaking views. Then it was back home, to continue sorting out and unpacking boxes. Things seemed to be going well.

We had arrived at the shop in August. Our wedding day was planned for October. We had to arrange for Gillian to go to Woking in time to get her dress fitted and be involved in the organisation of the day. We also had to work out how I would travel down to Woking nearer the day. Alan was looking after the shop while we were getting married. The day of our marriage in Woking (Surrey), it rained on and off all day with storm-force winds, which forced our wedding car to drive round the countryside dodging fallen trees – causing us to arrive late for the reception.

All went well until we arrived at the hotel, which Eileen and Bill had paid for. We checked in at the reception of the hotel. We got the keys to our room. When we saw the room, our faces dropped. There, dangling from the ceiling was the longest cobweb I had seen. On the bed, the counterpane had a large filthy red circular mark; you could not miss it. This was our wedding night! We had not asked for any fuss to be made; we just wanted a quiet night for ourselves.

We went to reception to tell the manger we were leaving. He offered to move us to a different room and we reluctantly agreed. It was a long walk to the new room. We noticed on the way that the hotel décor was as dingy as the room we had left. When we got to the new room, we were aghast to find the bedding turned back with a newspaper on the bed and a pair of shoes underneath. To make matters worse, there was a very loud rumbling noise, which got louder and louder. The man showing us the room explained. "It's only the train that goes over a wooden bridge outside your window. It stops running at 11.30pm."

Colin – Mr C&G Fifties (50–60 years)

We thought, *Let's get out of here.*

We promptly left, after complaining to the management that this was our wedding night. He said, "Nobody told me." We didn't think we needed to say as we did not want anything out of the ordinary, just a peaceful night with no fuss.

We left and headed for Southampton. Gillian knew of a hotel called the Post House and there was a happy end to the story. We got a lovely room and had the night we expected then stayed a couple of days – visiting the famous Ocean Village before returning to Woking, then on to Burnley. It was certainly a night to remember!

After a few weeks' trading, however, we noticed the takings seemed quite low in comparison to the figures we had seen. We had seen audited accounts before we bought the shop. We soon realised the accounts we had seen were not accurate. I could see now why Mrs Jones had left so quickly. We also noticed that an unhealthy element of local youths were hanging about the shop at night. Although they did not cause us any problems, they were very noisy. This made me feel nervous, as they were there every night. We felt relatively safe as no damage would be done to the shop while they were about, but I was still on edge.

I spoke to one of them, who was a customer and seemed to be the leader. He offered to have a word with them, but things didn't change much. Gillian had noticed I was getting uptight and kept telling me not to worry. I replied, "It's all right for you. You don't have to deal with it." As time went on, my paranoia got worse and I started to get niggled with her.

Gillian does not lose her temper very often. She has a knack of defending herself in a relaxed fashion, which at the time I found very annoying. It seemed there was no way out of the situation, with the problems outside the shop. In trying to run the shop, events took their toll on me. In a moment of peace, Gillian suggested I go to the doctor's, as it looked like there might be a parting of the ways for us. I had never considered the chance she had taken in leaving home and coming to a new place with me.

The doctor told me I was suffering from acute stress and very high blood pressure, and in need of urgent medication. The doctor prescribed tablets for me but said it was going to take a long time to get better. I had never thought this would happen to me. We had only been at the shop for eighteen months. We then decided to extend the takeaway side to include hot sandwiches and what they in the north call baps. It made some difference but not a lot.

Eileen and Bill came to visit and sensed I was not myself. They offered to look after the shop, so we could go away for a week to the Lake District, which they would kindly pay for. On the morning we were due to go, suddenly I could not get my breath. I sat down on a chair; I was too weak to get up. We were all worried about my state of health and the loss of the holiday. After sitting in the chair for about an hour, I suddenly got up and said, "Let's go."

Eileen, Bill and Gillian were taken by surprise at my sudden movement. I couldn't explain why I suddenly felt better. We survived the holiday with no further problems. It was nice to be able to relax away from the shop. Maybe it was the scenery or the picturesque views of lakes Coniston, Windermere and Ambleside that did it. The holiday seemed to have made a difference and the medication helped calm me. Then, a few weeks later, I lost all my energy again. I could not understand why this should happen again.

Jean called, saying that she and Mum were coming to visit, but Gillian told her I was unwell. They should leave the visit for now and Jean agreed. A few minutes later, Mum rang. She wanted to speak to me but Gillian refused. She said I wasn't fit to speak with anyone. Mum demanded to speak to me, so again Gillian repeated that I was too unwell. Mum kept insisting. "He's my son, I will speak to him." Gillian again said I couldn't speak. Mum kept on and eventually Gillian had no choice but to put the phone down and terminate the call.

When I was feeling better, I went to see Mum. She lost her temper, calling Gillian some nasty names. I left, and we didn't speak again.

As time went on, my health improved. The loss of energy didn't reoccur. The shop takings were no better. To make matters worse, a Kwik Save convenience store opened just down the road. We watched our usual customers walk by with their Kwik Save shopping. The writing was on the wall for us, and we then suffered a major break-in.

After putting a large notice on the door, announcing our

competitive prices, people could not wait until we reopened to get their shopping. Afterwards, we had two more attempted break-ins and in one attempt someone even tried to take out the window frames. That was the end of the road for us. We decided to close the shop.

Gillian offered to get a job somewhere to pay the bills and I agreed to do the same. We then decided to convert the shop back into a house. We closed the business in 1996, which was fortuitous because a few days later a car crashed into what had been the shopfront area. Luckily, we were in the back of the house. If we had still been open, we may have had customers at the time of the crash, possibly causing injuries or worse. The crash caused considerable damage to the house, at a cost of around £3,000. The insurance claim became a nightmare. They delayed rather than helped. The outside walls of the house had to be taken down and rebuilt, taking three months to do.

CHAPTER SEVEN

Colin – Mr Various & Councillor Colin Sixties (60–72 years)

∞

In 1997, Gillian got a full-time job in the cash office at WH Smith in Burnley. I took a job at a charity hostel in Blackburn, which was only part time but better than nothing. I worked in the kitchen as a food service attendant, with other duties including washing up, cleaning and tea-making. I quite liked working there and the other staff members were nice.

Being part time, I turned my attention to other things. Near our house there was a very large three-storey factory known locally as Pigeon Palace. It had been an old textiles mill and had closed many years back. It was now in a dilapidated state. Only the pigeons would make it their residence. Local youths used to hang around outside it, and inside, it was an absolute eyesore. A local lady and myself approached the council in an effort to get it demolished. We were persistent, going to the council offices a couple of times a week. After a while, the lady moved away but I kept on. In the end, it seems they were fed up seeing me. They eventually agreed to knock it down.

I also got involved in a few other local issues, like road traffic, after a child was knocked down near to the shop. I was back at the town hall, demanding road humps to slow down the traffic. My work was noticed by one political party. They asked me to stand as their candidate for the upcoming election. I agreed to stand even though I knew nothing about campaigning. I spent days and evenings out canvassing. I talked to anyone who would listen, gathering information from people about what they felt was important to them. I LOST at the next local election. The leader of that party was extremely rude to me for losing. I thought, *That was*

Colin – Mr Various & Councillor Colin Sixties (60–72 years)

a waste of time. I won't do that again. I can relax and put my feet up now.

Some months passed, then came a knock on the door from an opposing party. They wanted me to cross the floor and join them.

Muggins said, "Yes". I observed earlier that my brother was an attention seeker, yet it seemed I was ten times worse. I stood again at the next election and I worked just as hard as before. Guess what. Even with a couple of hundred pictures of yours truly pasted all over the area, and the assistance of a prominent MP, I LOST again!

I stood for the third time, taking another shot at it. This would be my LAST time. I tried to do something different – no pictures, no help, no knocking on doors. I just sat on my backside and hoped for the best. The surprising result was I WON! With a majority of 250 votes! I now became Councillor Colin Nightingale. This was destined not to last. I soon became disillusioned. I could not do what I believed in and had to toe the party line. I thought I had a brain of my own, yet was prevented from using it. I wasn't comfortable with the sniping at the Town Hall meetings. I was all right when the public attended, but after they left and we were tidying up the less important items, the cross-party mud-slinging started. It simply wasn't for me. I wanted to help people in the community and solve their problems. I had started to do that as an independent member of the public. I thought I could do even more as a councillor. How wrong I was.

In 1997, Gillian left WH Smith to take up a new post as a buyer for another firm on a decent salary. A year later, I left my job at the charity hostel. I rented a market hall café in Nelson, near Burnley. It seemed a good move as I liked cooking. I built up a regular clientele. I was kept busy most of the time, serving all-day breakfasts along with a comprehensive menu throughout the day. The market itself was a good old-fashioned market. It was large with lots of stalls. The stalls ranged from cheese to books, from fruit and vegetables to delicatessen, from butchery to sewing and knitting; in fact, everything you could want in one space. The stall holders were all friendly and knew their produce and how it could be used. If you had a question, they would have an answer. If they didn't know, they would know someone who did. It was that type of community. The market backed onto a nightclub, which was fine because the noise from the nightclub did not affect the market, which ran in the daytime. All seemed to be going well for about a year, but wait for it, one night the nightclub caught fire. The authorities had to close the market for safety reasons. I was concerned about my stock. I had to beg the authorities to be allowed in to clear perishable items. On arrival, there was another shock. The council workmen had broken down the door to my café, and a large amount of stock had been stolen. Obviously, I complained to the council. My complaint fell on deaf ears. I was forced to write to the council's ombudsman; there was no way I could take the loss of stock without compensation. My complaint was upheld. The council were forced to reimburse me and cover my losses. After all this aggravation and my general unhappiness in political correctness, I made the decision to resign as a councillor. My party were not happy with my decision and made me an appointment to meet a council official to discuss my situation. However, the official was more concerned about getting to watch his son play cricket than talking to me. He could not care whether I stayed or left. I was elected in 2000 and resigned later in 2000. I was out of work AGAIN!

Fortunately, after Gillian told her bosses what had happened, they offered me a job. It was initially as a labourer. After a short while, my duties improved after the firm decided they wanted to pack their own goods (nails, bolts and other items). The new job involved me prepacking all these items, so I could work through the list of items required and then stack the shelves. I enjoyed making the shelves look tidy and full. It seemed to help that one of the bosses knew I had been a councillor. Both Gillian and I were on good money and were able to accumulate some savings.

With both of our jobs going well again, we seemed to be on the up. So we put the house on the market and it sold in 2002. We knew before it was sold that we would have to find somewhere to live. I still had contact with some of my former council colleagues; one of them told me of a council property that was available in the Nelson area. I applied for the house. They granted me the tenancy. I found out later that my new abode had a history of bad tenants. As an ex-councillor, they knew I would be an ideal tenant. It needed a lot of work, but everything was sorted out. It's now a lovely

Colin – Mr Various & Councillor Colin Sixties (60–72 years)

semi-detached house in a nice area near to town. We didn't make a profit from the sale of the house. That did not matter. We were happy and we still live there more than twenty years later.

We have been happy, although we have had some serious health problems along the way. Gillian had to retire after being diagnosed with breast cancer. The first cancer needed an operation followed by chemotherapy and radiotherapy. The second needed an operation, then just chemotherapy this time. Cancer, twice in five years! This hit Gillian hard, and it didn't do a lot for me either. I did my best to make things easier for her. Being a man, it was hard to understand what she was going through. All I could do was to be there for her and do the house chores.

Slowly but surely, Gillian got better and was always there for me. Then it was my turn! I had retired at sixty-five, but to keep myself active I decided to try some voluntary work in a hospital. I had to go to head office. I needed to have a medical. An appointment was made for me to see their doctor. While sitting in the waiting room before seeing the doctor, I started to read the notices, on the notice board. One said, *Do you go to the toilet to pass water more than three times a night?*

I thought, *Yes, I do*. There were a number of other questions to which I thought,

Yes. I couldn't get it out of my mind. I passed my medical and went to work in the local hospital. Everything seemed okay.

I told Gillian what I had read at the doctor's. We agreed I should see my GP. He confirmed that I needed a check to see if everything was all right. I was told I needed to have a biopsy, so off I went to hospital – feeling somewhat apprehensive.

What happened next, I would not wish on my worst enemy. The doctor said, "This is going to hurt! Hold the nurse's hand as tight as you can." He said, "The first two samples are going to be painful. The next four will be not so bad." He was right! If it wasn't for holding the nurse's hand, I would have hit the ceiling.

On having the last one, I heard someone say, "He's bleeding." I was given a handful of cloths and told to get dressed and go home. I could hardly walk, but nobody tried to help me. I made my way to the car then Gillian drove us home.

I was in pain. When I got home, the car seat and my clothes were covered in blood. I would never go through that again. When my results came through, I had to see a doctor at the hospital. He confirmed I had prostate cancer. He would cut it out, or I could have radiotherapy. He said, "In my experience, it would be better to have it cut out, but go home and think about it. Let me know at your next appointment."

At my next appointment I saw a different doctor (that's par for the course, isn't it?), who said he would recommend radiotherapy. I told him what his colleague had said, but he told me not to take any notice. "He's a surgeon and they love cutting things."

I said, "Charming!" He explained that you had to be careful if you cut out the prostate because if you didn't get it right, you could easily nick something else and do more damage. (He was a real cheerful sod!)

He said, "If you have radiotherapy, I'll be with you all the way."

I talked it over with Gillian. She said, "Do what you think is right for you." Radiotherapy it was.

A few weeks later, I got a letter inviting me to the Rosemere Radiotherapy Unit in Preston. It seems they were trying out an idea of introducing new patients to look at the machines to put them at their ease before they start the treatment. Gillian and I went. We were shown the layout of the building, where the radiotherapy rooms were. We were shown the machines and what we had to do when we went in for the treatment. They put me in the machine and told me it would be painless, and it was. I felt better when we were offered tea and biscuits. We met the radiologist. This was the best thing we did, as it took all the fear out of me. We told the staff that we agreed this visit had made a great difference to how we viewed the treatment.

As a patient, you are in the radiotherapy machine for just a minute. You have four pen like dots on your body, which the machine hones in on; one on each side of your waist, one on your chest and one near your belly button. The machine gives fifteen seconds to each dot. I had to have this treatment every day for two months. The hospital provided transport there and back, with volunteer drivers, who were terrific. The treatment, as I said, was painless, but the cumulative effect takes its toll. You get very tired over the whole period.

The only thing I wasn't aware of was the pain when the treatment was over. I had trouble with my waterworks and couldn't stop wanting to pass water. Overnight, I went to the loo over 200 times. I would pass a little water then go back to bed, then immediately needed to get up to try again. It was no different during the day. A family friend brought me a portable loo, which they used in their caravan. It was a big help as we had a cubbyhole downstairs, so I didn't have to go upstairs every time. I knew things would get better eventually, so I kept a diary and crossed the days off until I got better. I had regular check-ups with the oncologist. I'm now on a drug called Tamsulosin, which I take every morning. I'm all right now and life is back to normal. Not everyone has the same reaction. I know some people who have not suffered at all.

Now we are both retired. I'm hoping there is nothing else. But, oh yes, there is!

I had a phone call from my sister, Jean, saying Mum was in hospital. This surprised me because I knew that Mum had made Jean promise not to let her be put in hospital. We collected Jean and we drove to the hospital. Mum was in a ward when we got there. Jean was upset because she felt that she had broken a promise.

As we got to Mum's bed, a young Asian nurse arrived and Mum shouted, "Get that bloody woman away from me." The nurse was led away in tears. She must have wondered what on earth she had done. I thought, *Here we go again. She's not happy unless she is shouting at someone.* If Mum was walking in a field, she would pick a fight with the birds for singing.

We left the ward, after being advised by the sister to see the registrar. He told us Mum hadn't got long to live. We left and went back to Jean's house to mull things over before returning home. The following day, we were called by the hospital, saying Mum had taken a turn for the worse. We picked up Jean and Alan and went straight to the hospital.

Mum appeared to be asleep. As we sat round the bed, a nurse brought us tea and biscuits. Then Alan broke the silence by dipping his biscuit in his tea. He opened his mouth to eat the biscuit; the soggy piece fell off and dropped into his teacup. Spontaneously, we all cracked out laughing. It's a good job Mum didn't see it.

After a while, visitors were entering the ward. It was a bit uncomfortable for us, as it seemed they were wondering why we were sitting around the bed. (I would have thought it was obvious.) I went to the ward sister and asked if Mum could be moved to a side room. She agreed, and Mum's bed was moved out of the main ward. We continued to sit round Mum's bed for a number of hours. Mum's breathing was slow but steady and a nurse told us we might be there for some time.

We decided to go home, collect some things and prepare for a long night's vigil. We also decided to get something to eat, as it was close to teatime. We stopped on the way home and bought fish and chips. After our meal, we went back to the hospital. When we got to the ward, a couple of nurses were crying. They told us Mum had died. We were amazed and went to see Mum's body. I said to Jean and Alan, "Well, maybe we can be a family again."

I couldn't help thinking, *Typical!* She had waited 'till we'd gone before passing on. She was cantankerous to the end. Purely from my point of view, I felt relieved after what she had put us through.

We arranged the funeral, which seemed strange because only half a dozen people would attend. Then we all went home to ponder the future. The funeral didn't go to plan because the vicar was drunk and could hardly stand up. His face was purple from the effects of his drinking, and he had trouble finding the buttons for the music. He had to lean on the pulpit to keep himself from falling over. We did thank him for his efforts. We were amazed that he managed to turn up in the state he was in. We made a complaint to the funeral directors but it fell on deaf ears, and Jean said, "Let's leave it." I knew she felt guilty for Mum being in hospital. Mum died in 2002 at the age of ninety-two, while I was sixty-four years young.

I sat down with Jean a few years later and she told me that both Alan and I were not wanted as children. It seemed Mum only wanted a girl. The reason was that Mum's mindset was (like a lot of mums) that because she looked after us as children through the Second World War, it was only right that as we got older, the children should look after her. That would be the role of the girl. Alan could go on his cycling trips to Devon and other south-west locations. I could go out and play football with friends – leaving Jean at her mercy. Being trapped at home, Jean was a prisoner to Mum's demands. She had never explained this to me or Alan.

Jean eventually told me how Mum had run her life into the ground. It left me feeling bad because I could have tried to help, had I known. In my late forties, I learnt that I had two other brothers, called Fred and John. I never met them, but I became aware of their existence. I learnt they were the children of my dad, James, from a previous relationship while he was very young. Jean and Alan told me that Mum had banned them from the house. She told Jean and Alan that the boys were wrong'uns, who had stolen from her. They would be a bad influence on us. Yet knowing that Mum only wanted a girl, it seems that when Dad died, she did not want his kids either.

I know that Fred and John lived in Newcastle. John died in his fifties. Jean was in contact with Fred in his later years. She asked if I would like to speak to him over the phone. I was surprised that she wanted me to speak to him after all these years. I agreed, while wondering what on earth I would say to him. I did ring him. We both found it difficult to make conversation.

I said to Gillian, "How do you feel about a trip to Newcastle?"

She wasn't sure but eventually said, "Okay".

Unfortunately, we never made the trip because Fred died a few weeks later at eighty-eight years of age. So ends another era.

Everything seemed to have settled down when Gillian asked me what I thought about a holiday abroad. I had to think about this, as I had never been abroad before. While we were both working, we had built up our finances. Neither of us smoked or drank or went out at night. We didn't have mobile phones with apps, or children, so we could afford a few holidays.

We booked a coach holiday to Germany. I won't fly anywhere in a tin can. If I'm going to die, I'll do it in my own time and not in anyone else's. Also, on a coach I can enjoy the scenery. I can enjoy the shops when we have a break on the journey.

Our coach took us through France and Holland, on our way to our hotel by the River Mosel. On our journey, we passed the Maastricht EU headquarters. It was not what I had expected. We were looking for an ultra-smart new building, but alas it was the opposite; it was hardly posh. Outside was a guard; a scruffy individual, with his uniform jacket undone, his hat on the back of his head and a cigarette hanging out of his mouth. His rifle was leaning up against the wall – a real worry for any terrorist! After we had stopped laughing, we were back to admiring the scenery. It was hot when we arrived at the hotel and the rooms were lovely. From our room we could see right across the River Mosel. After a pleasant evening, we had a good night's rest. In the morning, we opened the curtains to see a blizzard and about four inches of snow on the ground. We didn't mind. We had a good English breakfast. The waitress asked, "Do you want a glass of *apple saft*?"

I asked Gillian what it was and she said, "It's apple juice." I was introduced to my first word of the language.

On the coach with us were around twenty other people, including a young lady with a young boy aged around ten years old. This was about to add difficulty to the outing a few days later. Our coach driver was taking us to a location where the River Mosel meets the Rhine – a place called Koblenz. He assured us that even though it was cold, with snow still on the ground, there were places we could go. Most of us got on the coach. When we got to Koblenz, the driver said he would drop us off. He would collect us in a couple of hours. We arrived here early in the evening and went sightseeing. During this time, it got a lot colder and icy underfoot. We looked for somewhere warm with a bit of life. There were very few places open, and none of them allowed children. We had the lady with the little boy with us. We spent the evening walking around in the freezing cold.

We happened on a single-storey building advertising music and dancing. We thought we were in with a chance, only to find the place empty when we went in. Tempers were fraying as we returned to the spot where the driver was to collect us. We had to stand around for ages until he turned up. There was a stand-up row with the driver, and the atmosphere remained tense back at the hotel. After tea and hot drinks were had, we all calmed down and put it down to experience.

On Wednesday, after the snow had gone, the driver took us to town. We expected a trip round the shops to cheer us all up. When we arrived, the shops were shut! You couldn't make it up. The place was dead. The travel agents had not warned us when booking that when you go to Germany at Easter time, everything shuts. The only place you can visit is the graveyard. So, back at the hotel, we were feeling peed off.

We got an apology from the driver, who then remembered a place that would be open, run by an Englishman. I don't remember exactly where it was but we all had a good day out – including the little boy. The place was like a large open-air market near the river, where we could sit and drink coffee. It also had some small stalls offering good bargains.

It was a good holiday, in spite of the weather. We had seen some lovely scenery and the people seemed friendly – in spite of not meeting many of them. Looking back, I remember visiting the walled city of Trier. Our coach stopped there for around an hour. We looked around to find some great shops. Gillian and I were quite taken with the city. So much so that we almost missed the coach because we couldn't remember the way to the pick-up point.

Back in Koblenz, we visited the wartime statue of Kaiser Bill. The huge statue faced the confluence of the two rivers and was badly damaged by the allies. It was quite a sight! Before returning home, the coach stopped at a large duty-free area with various shops to get lots of beer and wine. The driver asked the passengers to say that it was theirs if challenged. We didn't ask any questions.

A few weeks after arriving home, things were getting back to normal. Work was needed on our garden, nothing too strenuous. I was aware of an ache above my left leg, but as it wasn't too painful I tried to ignore it. I thought I must have somehow pulled a muscle. As the days went on, I felt a small lump in my stomach, which then moved down into my groin. I was not good with pain and not comfortable going to the doctor's or anything worse. Gillian persuaded me to go to the doctor, saying it would get worse if I didn't get it seen to.

I plucked up courage to have a check-up, only to be told it was a hernia, which needed surgery. I was a bag of nerves on the day of surgery, and on arriving at Airedale Hospital (in Yorkshire), I told Gillian that I couldn't go through with it, saying, "Let's go home."

She firmly reassured me. "You are better than this."

I said, "Okay, let's do it."

I got into the ward and a nurse asked, "Can you walk to the theatre?"

I replied, "I hope it's a good film."

He said, "You bet."

I got onto the operating table and he gave me an injection then asked me to count to ten. I don't know how far I counted. The next time I woke up, I was in bed and was offered tea and toast.

A nurse then said, "Get dressed, you can go home, but take things easy." I didn't think I was fit to do much else! I had to walk down two flights of stairs to meet Gillian and get into the car. I had to be driven home. I'd had keyhole surgery. After two weeks of bed rest, I was back to my irritating best.

A few weeks later, we decided to try another holiday, this time in Cornwall. Gillian had seen an advert for a holiday complex at a place called Seaton. It looked ideal, by the sea. We booked and made the 350-mile trip, taking turns at driving. We drove about 80 miles each and, with some stops, our journey took six hours.

When we arrived, our flat was on the ground floor. Unfortunately, it didn't look great. It also felt a bit damp. It was late spring and there did not seem to be much in the way of heating. On the second day, I got up and went to wash. I noticed a horrible smell but couldn't locate it. After emptying the water from the sink, lo and behold, it came up the bath plughole. I said to Gillian, "That's novel."

We persevered but after breakfast we made a complaint at the site office. The receptionist was as useful as a chocolate fireguard. We got the usual "I'll speak to the site handyman." We never saw him.

On the Thursday, we checked out. We had had enough. We made our way out of the complex. When driving down the road, the heavens opened so we pulled into a nearby car park. Luckily, it was only a heavy shower. Gillian said, "We have plenty of time so I'll go for a walk to get some fresh air." I stayed with the car, not wanting to leave it, as it was full of luggage.

After a while, Gillian hadn't got back so I decided to go and look for her. There was no one around. I locked the car and set off to find her, not knowing which way to go. It didn't matter because I could now see her coming towards me. I wondered where she had been. She described walking up a steep hill and finding a large complex of holiday apartments.

She had gone to take a look.

There was a door marked Reception and once inside the man said, "Come in." He was the owner of a self-contained apartment complex, overlooking the sea and a long beach. It was so high up from the shore that Gillian could see the road we had travelled on. She said, "You will love it." We enjoyed our first holiday here and for the next four years stayed there twice a year.

We met lots of people and got on well with the locals. Seaton is a beautiful place, with a wildlife park just down the road from the complex. This park is about a mile long and a hundred yards wide, with streams and a large lake. There were ducks, swans, kingfishers and a variety of other different birds. We found it spectacular.

There was also a beach café, where we regularly enjoyed a Sunday roast. From the beach there was a lovely coastal walk, where we walked all the way to a little village called Downderry – about a mile from Seaton. We had tea in the small village café then visited the small shops before walking back to Seaton. We got on well with the café owners, Wendy and Robert, and also the owners of our accommodation, Mr and Mrs Stamp.

We enjoyed our stays at Mount Brioni (our accommodation) and would have recommended it to anyone. Thanks to Gillian's little walk, we had discovered a real gem.

One day, Gillian and I decided to have a day out in Blackpool. We set off and went via Lytham St Annes. We arrived in Blackpool. We walked along the promenade and looked in various shops. Later on, we spotted a fish and chip shop and went in for lunch. We took our time and had a coffee after the meal. A short while later, I started to feel a little unwell. I said to Gillian, "I need to go to the toilet quickly!" She let me know she had seen some public toilets just before we found the chip shop. Off I went at great speed. I found the loo, ran in and found an empty cubicle. I was sat down doing what was necessary, when I heard ladies' voices and a noise that sounded like wheels. As I sat there, I thought, *Silly women, they are in the wrong toilets.* It soon dawned on me; it was silly me that had not read the sign on the door. I thought, *What do I do now?* I sat there, quiet as a mouse, until I heard them leave. I put on a straight face, hoping no one would notice, and marched out, only to see a few women had gathered outside. I had not run in years, but I did that day. When I got back to Gillian, she asked, "What have you been doing? You look all in."

I said, "Don't ask." I recounted the story to her later; she roared with laughter.

CHAPTER EIGHT

Colin – Mr Bird Haven Seventies (72–81 years)

∾

In between our trips to Cornwall, I started suffering energy losses, such as I had experienced in the past. The spells didn't last long but were eventually concerning enough to put an end to our Cornish holidays. My health concerns were now against the trips, and as time went on, the spells were getting worse. They were sometimes so serious that I had spells in hospital and had to wear a blood pressure monitor on some occasions.

The monitor didn't register any details of the cause. After my fourth hospital stay, the consultant said he was going to take a gamble and fit a pacemaker. After this was done, the other men in the ward, being a friendly group, named me Gerry (Gerry Marsden having been the lead singer of the Pacemakers – a Liverpool pop group).

My pacemaker was fitted in March 2013, at the grand young age of seventy-five. It seemed to work as my energy levels were gradually restored. With the help of medication. I did get the odd dizzy spell, but nothing that worried the doctors. I put them down to old age.

As things got back to normal, Gillian and I decided to go to a local auction in Burnley. A decision that brought another change to our lives. We went there to view the lots, as we did on occasions to find the odd bargain through the auction. One day, we pulled up in the car park. I saw two lads cutting the grass. I suggested to one of them that they could do with some bird feeders hanging up in a few places. He mentioned there was some derelict land, which would be perfect for that. I told him I would love to set up a place with some feeders. He said, "Why don't you ask if that is possible?" If you don't ask, you will never know, and Gillian was keen to get involved, so, here we go!

I was very nervous walking to the owner's office. I asked the owner's wife if she would let us use a piece of the land to put up bird feeders. She responded, "You are just the people I want, I love wildlife." She showed us around and offered a decent square of land, beside the Leeds and Liverpool Canal, with a large wooded area close by. There were all kinds of birds: from nuthatches to woodpeckers, along with the occasional kingfisher, besides the usual garden birds. Gillian and I set about clearing the land and making it look nice. The owners came to look and seemed to come to the conclusion that we were not there to mess about.

We did a deal with the owner, Mark, and Laura, who owned the auction centre and who offered a discount in the café for food and cups of tea. We met lots of people while in the café, who would ask about what we were doing. Many kind people brought food for the birds and others made donations. Gillian came up with a name for our project; we named it 'BIRD HAVEN'.

Bird Haven entrance. As we look towards the trees, we can see some birdfeeders and a nesting box on the tree. There is also a bird table. On the right, we can see the Leeds and Liverpool Canal

Bird Haven entrance. As we look into the Haven, we can see flowerbeds in front and to the side. Birdfeeders to the left and bird table on the right. There is also a chair for visitors

The bird haven was started at the beginning of May 2011 with a small area of land. We put up birdfeeders, some of which were donated, and with an assortment of food for different species, we were encouraged to see many birds coming regularly. We started to clear the rubbish from this area. We progressed and developed about 200 yards of ground. We created a pathway through the wooded area and had plans to plant this with bluebells, snowdrops, daffodils and other wild flowers. We also made three flowerbeds from donated wood. These were planted to encourage insects, bees and butterflies. The bird haven project at this stage consisted of just this piece of land. Little did we know what it would become in the future.

Colin – Mr Bird Haven Seventies (72–81 years)

Bird Haven. I am at the entrance looking into the Haven. The path is edged with wooden poles. Another bird table is on the right. If you look carefully, halfway down on the right is an old railway line from the days when the site was a coal mine

Bird Haven. Our new flowerbed is in place. It is edged with wooden poles and planted with flowers to encourage insects

The owners of the auction, having seen our work, gave us permission to extend our project. They gave us the green light to progress further along the land but to stick to the edge along the canal. We started to research the land's previous usage. We didn't know that the auction house was built on the well-known Bank Hall Colliery, which had shut down some fifty years ago. The mine shafts stretch under Burnley in all directions. Some as far as Hapton, some 5 miles away, where in the 1960s there was a mining disaster, killing and injuring many brave miners. Back at our plot of land we uncovered part of a railway line, which we later cut out. We met an old miner who used to work there. When we were clearing the land, he showed us where the old coal sheds had stood. Now everything was hidden under trees and bushes.

The land that we had been given to use was full of potential but had been unused for many years. It had originally been part of a coal mining site then was used more recently as a BMX cycle centre. It had then been left unused and was consequently overgrown with vegetation and covered in rubbish of all kinds.

Our outlook for Bird Haven was already changing from a small 200-yard project to something far more substantial. We created a vision of what the future could be.

*

What is Bird Haven?

Bird Haven is an area developed to encourage birds and wildlife by providing food and habitat for them to thrive.

What is the purpose of Bird Haven?

To transform unused land into a natural habitat for birds and wildlife and to create a space where people can come and enjoy the natural environment while watching the wildlife.

Colin – Mr Bird Haven Seventies (72–81 years)

What is the future vision for Bird Haven?

We wish to create a circular nature trail on the site, creating areas for butterflies, bees and other animals as well as wild birds. We hope also to develop areas of natural planting using wild flowers and woodland plants, all with a view to provide as natural a habitat as possible. There is no charge for people to come and enjoy the site. Indeed, we hope that everyone will come and enjoy what the site has to offer.

*

Bird Haven entrance

We progressed a little further along in the hope that we could make a pathway through the next area. In time, our pathway began to take shape. Some parts of the ground were so slippery that it was hard to stop our feet sinking in the mud. We needed a solution.

We went to the local builders' merchants not far from the site, for advice on what to use on the path. It was decided to use 2-inch stone. We bought a 20-tonne load of 2-inch stone. It was delivered and tipped onto the ground near the entrance.

I wondered, *How am I going to shift this lot?*

As luck would have it, the answer appeared in the shape of a very large man. I had seen him a few days earlier but had not taken any notice of him. I was naturally wary, as he looked like a Hell's Angel without his bike! He asked, "Do you need any help?" As a single parent to a little boy, he couldn't get employment because no boss would give him the necessary time off to collect his son from school. He also had no one to look after him after school.

The unlikely angel of mercy was called Larry. Together, we started on with the heavy work. After a few days, while sitting in the café eating lunch, another man asked if we had any work going. This man was called Martin and he had an autistic son called Sam. Martin explained that Sam kept looking at the pile of stones near the entrance. I was surprised and responded, "If you can start moving them, I'd be very grateful." Martin told Sam and he was very pleased.

Martin and Sam came for one day a week. They had their own wheelbarrows and shovels. Sam had his name on his barrow, which he was very proud of. They barrowed the stones from the entrance to the path area, then Larry and I started to lay the path – adding extra stones to the slippery part where necessary.

One day, Larry suspected we had unwanted vandals on the site, saying, "Come and look at this."

He took me to see about ten stones on a bench. I wondered, *Who would do that?* Larry suspected local kids. I had to agree. A few days later, I was telling Martin about the stones.

I explained to Martin that Larry had discovered the stones on the bench. He started to roar with laughter. He said, "It's not the kids, it's Sam." He explained that every time Sam took a load of stones to the site of the path, he put a stone on the bench. After he had done ten trips, he knew it was time to go for a cup of tea and some toast, before going home.

I said, "That's fair enough." I went to explain it to Larry.

We spent some weeks following the routine of the stones and the path. The path was taking shape and beginning to look quite professional.

A few months later, we had to say farewell to Larry. He had decided to leave Burnley for pastures new. He had been a valuable asset to us and had helped tremendously with the heavy work. I tried to contact him a few times to see how he was getting on, but without success. Now it was a case of carrying on without Larry.

Land before the digger came

Digger in action

The path we had made ran close to the canal for about 200 yards, before turning sharp left alongside a 10-foot-high palisade metal fence. The terrain close to this fence was impassable – full of concrete slabs, girders and uneven, slippery grass. After speaking with Gillian and Mark, we decided together to hire a digger, complete with driver, to clear all the debris and rubbish, leaving an area of about 10 feet (about 3 metres), so that we could continue the path. We met the digger driver. I asked him if his machine could handle the terrain. He said his machine could handle anything – even this uneven land.

Several days later the digger man duly arrived. Halfway through the job, the digger lost its caterpillar track, causing it to slip down a slope and crash into a fence. The air was blue! "Look what's happened to my [so-and-so] digger," he fumed. He was still swearing half an hour later and was yelling so loudly that he could be heard 50 yards away.

In the end, I told him to calm down. I reminded him that he had said his digger could handle anything. He carried on, so I told him I wasn't paying to hear his ranting. If he couldn't do the job, I would find someone else. This had the desired effect and he quietly carried on and finished the job. He actually did a good job in the end, with no further problems.

The path was now extended. We could look through the metal fence. We saw what appeared to be a waterfall. It turned out to be an overflow from the canal, in case the canal level got too high. There was also a river nearby, running through the park. These features were about 40 feet (about 12 metres) below. We were surprised to find we were so high up.

Our planned path extended about another 50 yards, so our nature trail was getting longer. When the extended path was completed, we encountered some very tall trees. We had to cut a narrower section of the path around them. There was not much room to work, so we had to cut a winding path around the trees. This made the nature trail seem more authentic.

It took at least six months to dig out around 20 yards of clay, with boulders mixed in it. Fortunately, again, we got some extra help from a local community group. They happened to come along

Colin – Mr Bird Haven Seventies (72–81 years)

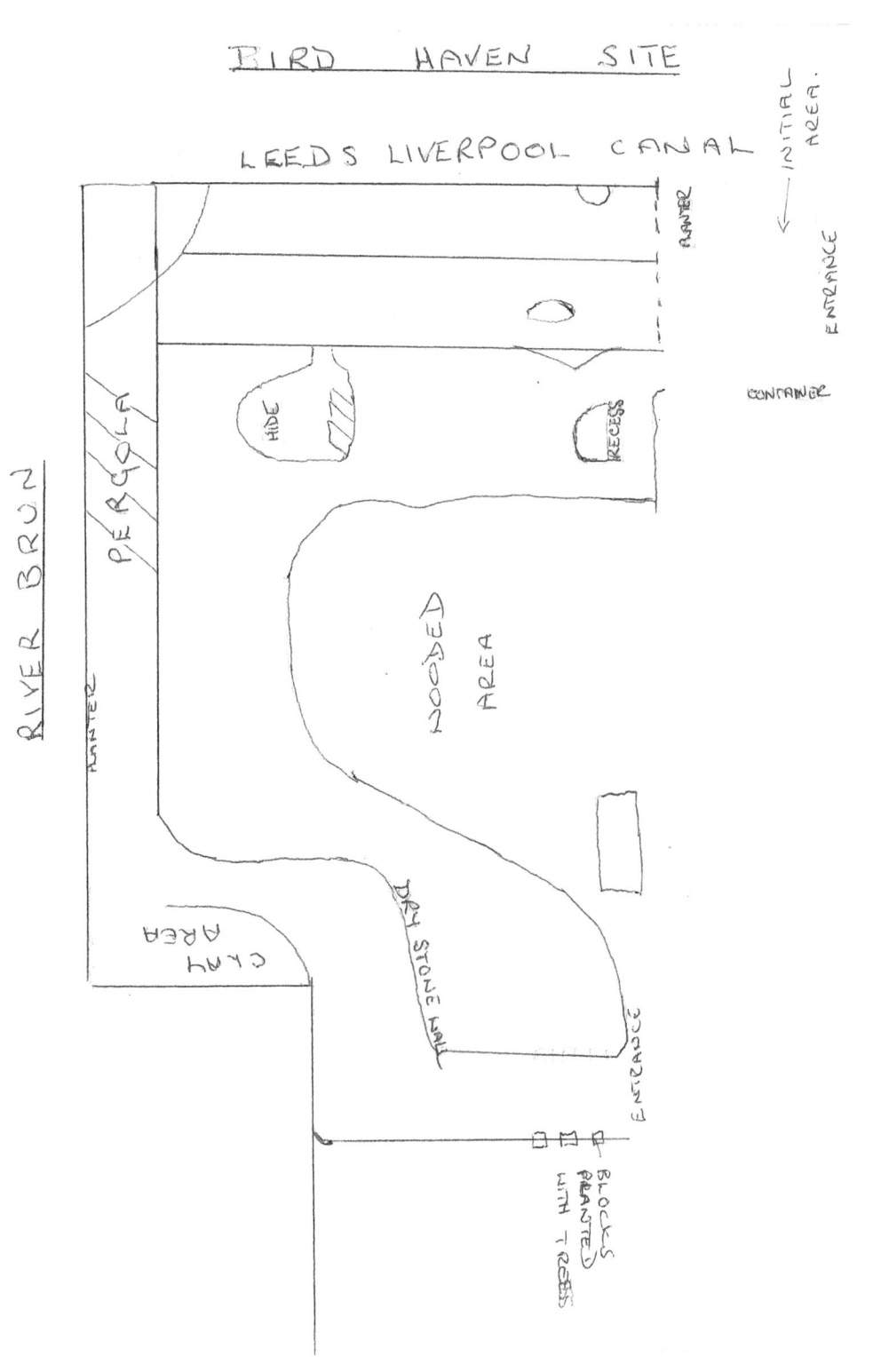

BIRD HAVEN SITE

after hearing about the work we were doing. Thankfully, they stayed long enough to help us move the clay and to see the job through.

After Sam had finished moving the stones, he started to move the surplus earth, including the clay. We were moving into the winter period and Gillian asked Martin if we could take some photographs of Sam working. Martin agreed but warned us, "Don't let Sam see you, because he doesn't like having his picture taken."

Gillian hid behind some bushes and captured some photos in secret. She had them printed and gave them to Sam as a Christmas present. He absolutely loved them. He proudly showed the pictures to the auction room and café staff. Shortly after Christmas, Sam and Martin left us. They had visited a farm on the days they were not working with us and Sam loved the pigs. He wanted to do some work at the farm and see the pigs. Again, we were thankful for their invaluable work and said we would always be pleased to see them, when they came to visit. We are still friends with Martin, Sam and his mother, Bernadette, and it will always remain that way for us.

We were lucky enough to have made contacts with many local businesses. The builders' merchants was one; the manager there was very interested in what we were doing and gave us a lot of advice on what to use for different projects. Another business we had contact with was a fencing company, who we had both worked for previously and had kept close contact with after we left their employment. This was to prove beneficial to us. The owner was also interested in wildlife and came to visit our site. He donated a large quantity of wood for us to use. It was all damaged or unsaleable wood but it was useful to us for making items such as bird boxes, bird tables initially and other things. It would be delivered in a short while, when it was sorted.

From time to time, we walked around the auction centre on viewing days, looking at the items for auction. We bought a lot of cheap items that would suit the nature trail. On one of these viewings, a man approached and asked me about Bird Haven. We showed him around and he asked if he could be part of the team. He looked like a cowboy, and it was no surprise when he told me that he performed at Wild West re-enactment shows, touring the north west.

He was small in stature, with grey hair, so we named him Stumpy, after a character in the Western film *Rio Bravo*, starring John Wayne. He really took to his new name and liked what we were doing. He turned up early each day and got stuck in – taking a lot of weight off my shoulders.

On the site, there were hundreds of bricks and large chunks of concrete. Stumpy kept asking if he could build some walls around the site. I politely declined, suspecting he couldn't do it. Sensing that he was upset with my answer, I asked Gillian what she thought, and she said, "Why not let him try? Let him build a small wall. If he gets it wrong, so be it." When I told Stumpy, his face lit up.

Stumpy's dry stone wall

Rustic table made from tree stumps and wood

One of our fences made from donated wood

I explained to Stumpy that we wouldn't be on site the next day; we had a meeting to go to. When we returned, he said, "Come and see what I've done. I hope you'll like it." He led us round the nature trail and I couldn't believe my eyes! He had built a wall about 30 yards long and 4 feet high, with a mixture of small and larger stones. It was a real beauty, and I remembered the old adage, never judge a book by its cover.

I told Stumpy, "You can build walls wherever you think it will benefit the site," and he did.

My meeting a few days earlier had been successful, so I told Stumpy I needed him early the next morning for an expected delivery. When he saw what arrived, he exclaimed, "Where did you get that **** lot from? [or something similar] Look at all that **** wood!" There was over a tonne of wood in various shapes and sizes. The first thing we had to do was to sort it into pieces of the same size. The amount of wood we had meant this was going to be no small task. We worked hard to sort the load. We were then able to see exactly what we had and decide how to use it. We were about to start making fences in a big way. We thought we could put fences along the path on each side. This would not have been an option before we received this delivery. It would have cost far too much. We then had another pleasant surprise: Stumpy was good at woodwork. He could not wait to get started. With walls going up and fences being made, I was happy, and in our few breaks, we would sit on our newly made benches – another of Stumpy's creations – to have a cup of tea and watch the birds.

We decided to make some planters with the wood. We had a range of sizes of wood so consequently the planters ranged from 2 foot by 2 foot square ones to very large ones, 8 or even 12 foot long by 3 to 4 foot wide. Some were even more abstract in size and shape, depending on the wood we used. Each of the planters could be made to fit the place on the site that it was going.

Wooden planter made from donated wood

I had noticed that the large birds, particularly wood pigeons, were eating most of the bird seed and pushing out the small birds. I found four very large concrete blocks and a large oblong coal bunker which I placed on top of the blocks in an upright position. On top of that, I laid two long scaffold boards horizontally. I then bought a large metal pet cage and secured it onto the boards. The little birds could now squeeze through the wires and the big birds could not get in.

I rigged this up and sat on the bench to see what happened. Before very long, the cage was full of different species: from bullfinches to nuthatches. What a result! After this success, I put up another five of these cages at various points along the trail.

The wood we had donated came in very handy for many things. Not only did Stumpy make many fences around the site, he also helped build what we called the recess.

Colin – Mr Bird Haven Seventies (72–81 years)

Bird feeder for small birds

The Recess made from donated wood

This was a shelter put up so visitors could sit and watch the birds even when it was raining or windy. There was a bench inside made by another supporter of the project. There was also a rustic table made from fallen tree trunks on the site, which was useful if you had a drink or other items with you. The recess looked out over one of our bird cages and further over to the woodland beyond.

Another structure we built was the hide. Again, we had help from another woodworker and friend. This was made from our stash of wood. It was the size of an 8 foot by 6 foot shed. It had a door at the back and a window at the front with flaps to open each section. Inside was a bench near the window. Bird watchers could sit inside and have one or more flaps open to see the birds. Outside, the hide feeders were mounted on poles set up in ranch style.

The Hide with viewing flaps open

Feeding station seen from the hide

Along the metal-fenced area across the end of the plot we decided to erect a pergola. We were keen to make a structure that we could use to train plants on. This seemed to be a suitable place. We used some of the very long planks and poles to create the pergola; some poles were bedded into the ground and others were secured to the metal fence. In time, the trees that were overhanging became entwined with the planting and created a very natural-looking feature.

The Pergola

We had been here now for almost five years and the nature trail was open for visitors. Bird Haven was always a hobby for us which we funded ourselves. Any donations we got were much appreciated. We also had our own T-shirts and sweatshirts printed with *Bird Haven* on them, which we proudly wore on our promotional and fund-raising events, of which there were many. There was no entry charge but we put up post boxes for donations. If people donated, that helped to pay for the tonne of birdseed we bought each year. If they didn't donate, we hoped they'd enjoyed their visit and would come again. Being able to build Bird Haven was a pleasure for us, and changed me completely. Even though there were a few ups and downs, I was more relaxed than I'd ever been. Even Gillian noticed the change in me. When we started the project, we could not have realised how large it would become and how beneficial it would be for everyone who worked on it and for those who visited.

Over the years, we had help from a lot of people, sometimes for a day, sometimes for a couple of days, and other people stayed for some months. On one occasion, we had an offer from a firm that looked after foreign students. They asked us if we could find work for about a dozen French students for one day. We said yes and agreed to meet the organisers the following morning. We worked on a plan so that small groups could work together, each group with a person who had a little English.

When they arrived, I decided to show them around the nature trail. I could not speak a word of French but fortunately most of them could speak a little English. They followed Gillian and me along the path. I had to turn around and talk to them while walking along. In not looking where I was going, I stepped off the path and tripped over a tree root – making a fantastic dive through the air and landing flat on my face. I jumped up immediately (in true Del Boy fashion – of *Only Fools and Horses* fame), shaking my head and taking an 'I'm not hurt' stance. I could hear the students laughing and I heard a broken English voice say, "Look! Tom Daley!" To which both Gillian and I started laughing. It was a good start and broke the ice on a very productive day. The students worked hard and did anything we asked of them. We had stops for drinks and then for lunch. Luckily, the weather was good enough for us to get the work done. We enjoyed their company even though there was not much conversation owing to the lack of a common language. The day ended well; we wished them a good stay and hoped they had enjoyed themselves. We went home, both of us tired and me somewhat sore from my fall.

A few days later, a friend of the family, Geoff, joined us. He was working with another community group, which had unfortunately folded through ill health of the organiser. He came to see what we were doing and wanted to help. A fresh face came at the right time, as Stumpy wanted to leave to try something else. It was sad to see him go, as he had put so much time and effort into seeing Bird Haven achieving the success it deserved. He had built excellent dry-stone walling and his woodwork was second to none. Some of his quaint fences caught the eye. To me, they were his masterpieces.

We were sorting out the flowers for Gillian to plant, as she was very good and knowledgeable on the subject. She loves gardening and was full of good ideas (a lot better than me). Geoff helped her out whenever needed.

As we were sorting out the plants, I noticed four people standing by the canal on the other side, looking around. There were two men and two women. I said, "Hello". They told me they were looking at the canal to see if an unused inlet could be used as a dry dock for barge repairs. The inlet they were viewing was an old canoe centre, which had closed down many years ago.

As you drove over the canal bridge into the auction house car park, the offshoot of the canal ran close by. It was about 60 yards long and filled with all sorts of rubbish. It looked like a cesspit because people just threw whatever they wanted in it. I commented that it would take some clearing out, but they said it wouldn't be a problem to them. Apparently, they had already applied for planning permission and were told it would be granted. One of the men was Leonard and the other was called Bill.

A further year went by then Mark from the auction house told me that Leonard was bringing in lorries and other heavy equipment for excavation work. Mark had given Leonard permission to use the car park.

A few months later, the excavation started, which was good for him but not for us. One morning, we were sitting having a cup of tea on site, when we became aware of some unwanted visitors in the form of hundreds of rats. We sat in our newly built hide watching our four-legged friends running about, climbing the trees and eating the bird seed. They were everywhere! Even when we were walking down the paths, they ran past us.

Mark came to see me and said that some of the auction visitors were complaining about the rats on our nature trail. I asked him what he thought I should do about it. He said, "I don't know, but you've got to do something. It won't be long before they are running about in my café." I managed to buy some rat poison blocks from a local farm suppliers, but it was a waste of time and money. So the next thing I decided to try was to stop feeding the birds.

I had a visit from Leonard, to apologise for the trouble. He said if there was anything he could do to help, I only had to ask. We decided to close the nature trail for at least a fortnight but check the situation each day. It took almost three weeks to get back to normal and reopen.

Double concrete blocks planted with native trees

Path made from donated scaffold boards

I was becoming really friendly with Leonard and his team. One day, he called me over and said he had something for me. While cleaning out what was to be his dry dock, he had uncovered about 200 double concrete blocks. He brought them down to me on his forklift truck. He helped me place them in a curved line as a path edging. Gillian and I took a trip to a local garden centre and bought a load of small native trees. These were planted in the block squares. These trees would grow to a height of 6 feet. This would be a feature at the other end of the nature trail.

After we had planted the blocks with the small trees, we had just one more area to finish leading to the blocks and trees. It was an area of path about 100 yards long. It had one of Stumpy's dry stone walls along the side but was prone to flooding regularly. I decided to lay a pathway that was raised up with wooden cross pieces. On top we laid scaffold boards that another local firm had donated to us. Then we put chicken wire on this so that people did not slip on it. On this pathway we could now put some seating and planters. Also in the trees we had some bat boxes put up.

Even though Leonard faced a monumental task at his dry dock, he always found time to spend with us. He brought us all sorts of things he had dug up, which would look authentic on our trail. It took some time before the dry dock was opened. We were invited to the official opening. There seemed to be a lot of important people there.

A year later, when Gillian and I went to feed the birds, we were shocked at what we saw. Originally, when Mark and Laura had given us permission to start the bird sanctuary, the understanding was that we could use the land alongside the canal until such time as Mark wanted to use it himself. We knew that when that time came, we would need to move off. He had also assured us that when that was to happen, he would let us know in advance. We had always had a good relationship with him (which has continued to this day) but we were shocked to find a very large digger cutting a large swathe of trees down.

I went to see Mark, who told me he had a new partner who wanted to use the land. I questioned why he didn't tell me in advance as he had promised. He reassured us that we could stay. Gillian and I decided to see what happened next. A few days later, as we went to feed the birds, there were men with chainsaws cutting down the trees. Mark's new partner (who I knew) said his lads were only taking out a few trees. Any damage done to our nature trail, he would put right.

Things did not get any better. We walked round the nature trail and our hearts sank. Fallen trees had damaged our fences; large boards were leaning against our pergola and Stumpy's brick walls were damaged. I spoke to Mark and showed him the damaged fences. He said, "They're not that bad." His new partner didn't want to know. So that was it! A nice project came to an abrupt end.

Fundraising for Bird Haven

Fundraising in fancy dress

Fundraising for Bird Haven

Woodpecker at Bird Haven

We sold off everything we could and managed to make a few bob back, leaving what we couldn't move where it was. Perhaps someone else could restore it. It was difficult for me to accept that I was too old to do the necessary repairs. I was nearing my eightieth birthday and needed to take stock of my life.

I would like to tell you about a coincidence and sequence of events that you could not make up. It concerns an event which I wrote about in Chapter Three. I described entering a dance competition with my sister, Jean, where we had to do the jive. We were awarded third place; we never knew who came first because we had only just moved to the area and did not know anyone. Little was I to know that some fifty years later I would meet the gentleman who won first prize.

While working at Bird Haven, I had been going to Burnley matches at Turf Moor. On one of these occasions, I entered a competition to guess the attendance at the match. I won and the prize was a tour of Burnley Football Club and a crate of beer, which (as I don't drink) I gave away. As we were being shown round Turf Moor, a man I recognised from his playing days came up to me and said hello. He went on, "I recognise you. You were in a dance competition a long time ago with a pretty young lady. You came third and I won first prize." I was gobsmacked. How could this man recognise me some fifty years later? The man was an absolute gentleman and was now an ambassador for the club. His name was Willie Irvine, Burnley and Irish International centre forward, famous in the '60s and played alongside Andy Lochhead, who I had met in club life with a lot of other players.

After Bird Haven, we needed to make life more relaxing for both myself and Gillian. However, as usual, there was another crisis coming along.

CHAPTER NINE

Colin – Mr Eighties (82–the present)

∽

The bad news was that Gillian's mother, Eileen, had passed away peacefully, but her husband, William, was struggling to look after himself, but was doing his best. We knew that he and Eileen went out as often as they could, visiting places like Towneley Park in Burnley, meeting regularly with a group of friends in the café. They also liked to go on holiday, especially to Llandudno in North Wales. They had both regularly attended church, and this was very important to them.

We often took Bill on holiday to Llandudno because it was a place he really loved, with fond memories. Gillian and I grew to like going there. After losing Bird Haven, we tried to go twice a year. We had a favourite hotel, called the Merrion, close to the pier and overlooking the sea. The town centre was compact, with everything we needed on hand, and we always went out for Sunday lunch.

As time progressed, Bill found it hard to get along, so we got him a walking frame. Although it slowed him down, he was determined to get wherever he wanted to go. The more he got used to it, the quicker he went, which didn't help the unsuspecting public who got in his way.

Back home, we both took Bill out for coffee in the week. On Saturdays, Gillian took him to Towneley Park to have coffee with the group of friends he had previously met with Eileen. He was happy being taken out and was always ready when he knew we were coming for him. It didn't last, as Bill was starting to struggle when he was at home. He had a nice bungalow, which he and Eileen had worked hard to get. He became a worry for us as his memory was not what it was. Remembering to take his medication at the right time was proving a worry. There was also the worrying possibility that if he put his dinner in the oven, would he forget that it was cooking?

Bill was not a silly man. In fact, it took me a long time to discover that he had a great sense of humour and was a very cheeky chappie. For his ninetieth birthday, we took him on holiday again to Llandudno and the hotel staff made him a cake. He was chuffed when he was blowing out the candles and the staff sang, "Happy Birthday" to him.

We found it difficult to look after Bill, as Gillian needed to get up very early to check on him and give him his tablets. He found it hard to remember to take them and often said he had taken them when he hadn't. We were also worried about him falling over and the risk of him being hospitalised. We both realised we could not give him the care that was needed. We had a chat with him about selling his bungalow and moving into a care home. He wasn't too sure about this idea but realised he would get the care he needed. We said we would arrange with the care home for us to take him out to Towneley twice a week, and he was happy with that idea. In fairness, he settled in well and enjoyed teasing the staff. It was almost a year later when he passed away peacefully in his sleep.

We managed to sell the bungalow a couple of weeks after he went into the care home. The money from the sale paid for his care home fees (about £700 per week). His passing came just before the coronavirus pandemic started, which in one respect was good. He would have found it hard to understand why we could not see him or take him out as usual.

During the pandemic was like no other time we had experienced, much like the war was to the previous generation. We had what was called LOCKDOWN, which meant we had to stay at home, apart from one hour a day when we were allowed out for exercise. We had to wear facemasks to protect others from the virus and had to be careful to wash our hands regularly and use hand sanitiser at all times when we were out. The other thing was to keep our distance from other people, to minimise the contact between people. The mantra was HANDS FACE SPACE. This was repeated regularly in daily press broadcasts which kept us updated with numbers of cases in hospital and deaths from the virus. We also had to SHIELD, which meant be even more careful. This was for people of young or old age and also those with specific health conditions. Everywhere was closed with the exception of food shops and chemists. This lasted for approximately twelve weeks, after which things were opened very gradually. We still had to wear facemasks and only go out when necessary. Hospital staff had to wear protective clothing and masks. Many people were hospitalised and many lost their lives. The pandemic lasted for about two years. Even now, the virus is still present, but we are told that we have to learn to live with it.

I would now like to refer back to Chapter Two where I spoke about going into the RAF, but Mum would only allow that if I went into nursing. At the time, I did not know why Mum had said that to me and what her motivation was for me to be a nurse. I have only recently found out the reason for this. After Mum died, my sister, Jean, had the task of going through Mum's papers. She found a letter dated January 1955, and titled COLIN THIRDE INCARNASCOPE, from a lady who was into reincarnation. This letter detailed things both in my past, what I would do in this life, and in the future according to her reincarnation beliefs. Mum, being into spiritualism, as I wrote in the early chapters of my book, also believed what this lady had written. A full copy of the letter is printed in the book, but I will highlight what I found to be interesting and relevant.

The first thing to mention is about me being a doctor or going into nursing. This was the reason for Mum's insistence that I went into nursing if I joined up. To her, it did not matter that I had no interest in nursing. In fact, the only time at that stage in my life I spent any time in a medical situation was when I had the motorbike accident and was in hospital for several months.

The second thing in the letter, which has actually happened, is that I strive to be the best at what I am doing, which I have mentioned in the book. It is open to interpretation whether this is to do with the letter or just a fact of life.

Thirdly, the letter states I will have to work hard to get on and will have to fight to succeed and will have many ups and downs along the way, ROLLERCOASTER COLIN.

Lastly, the letter states I will live a long life. Again, I leave it up to you whether the letter dictates this or whether it is just life itself and how you cope with it. One thing I would like to add is that when Mum received the letter, she could have shown it to me to justify what she wanted, but she chose not to. It is only now in my eighties that I am able to read the letter and understand why this was important to her. Now with hindsight, I don't think it would have made any difference.

It is now 2022 and I have reached my eighty-fourth birthday and we are wondering what lies ahead. My life has been a rollercoaster, with some good times and some disasters, yet somehow I have managed to fight my way through. But for the help of my wife, Gillian, over the last thirty-three years, I'm not sure where I would be today.

Thoughts

Up and down around I go,
Whatever's next I do not know.
Will it be good, will it be bad,
Is it fun or is it sad?
Who know what the future holds,
Stand tall and face what will unfold.

CHAPTER TEN

Mr Colin Conclusions

∞

Our childhood, during the war, was like that of many other children born at this time. We did not know any different. Our parents were making do, not having anything new; hand-me-downs and mended items were normal. Obviously, our parents had the worry of what was going on and they did their best to keep it from us children. Later on in life, you realise that our childhood was different from that of other generations, but to us it was normal.

Another thing you notice later in life is that your life can follow a very different course to others. I now know people of my age that have had only one or two jobs in their working life, whereas I changed jobs many times, mainly because I wanted to gain experience in as many areas as possible. I always say that I went to the university of life and am proud of that. I think now there will be no one that will have one or two jobs in a lifetime of work.

I look back now and wonder if my mother was just a product of her upbringing – strict and ruthless in everything – or whether losing her first husband early and remarrying resulted in her dislike of so many things. I wonder also if her dislike of so many people resulted in the family fragmenting at times, each person relying on their own resources rather than sticking together.

I think I have changed tremendously through my life. I started being very introverted, so afraid of my own shadow that I suffered bullying from an early age, both at home and at school. As I grew older, I managed to avoid situations where I could be bullied. I think this was more by luck than judgement.

As I grew older, I wanted to be part of a group, so I decided to dress and act to conform. However, I also wanted to stand out a little by being a bit more flamboyant, sometimes wearing colourful socks or carrying a colourful handkerchief. How this happened I'm not quite sure. I think, in a way, being repressed as a child, there was a bit of rebellion against the establishment. My time in the clubs saw me transformed into a confident person. I had to dress the part and wanted to be the best at everything. I worked hard to that end. I was comfortable and at ease in that environment. The same could be said of my time at Belle Vue. It was something different again, but I worked hard to be accepted and to be the best at what I was doing. I think from my late teens onwards, my own principle was to work hard and try to be the best I could. I developed a determined streak to get on.

In later life, I feel my character has mellowed. I still have the drive to be good at whatever I am doing at the time, but I am a bit more relaxed about being the best. I am happy about doing what I can to the best of my ability, but it does not mean I necessarily need to be number one.

My time at Bird Haven gave me a more relaxed perspective on work and life in general. The time to do things does not have to be now; it can be tomorrow or even next week. Watching the wildlife, the birds and the plants makes you take stock and be a little more patient both in what you need to do and in life.

The process of writing this book has also encouraged a feeling of taking time to get things right. It has been a far longer process than I had imagined, but at each stage it has been good to take a step back and review regularly how it is proceeding. I think I have also learnt that criticism can be both good and bad. When I was at school, I could only see the teacher marking everything down. I did not imagine that this might be to help me to do better next time and that comments made were to encourage and not to demoralise. During the writing of this book, I have learnt that criticism from others as well as your own can be used to improve what you are doing as well as to stimulate your own thoughts as to improvements you can make. I think these are life lessons as well.

I sometimes wonder what our lives would have been if we had had the knowledge of a lifetime's experience when we were young. However, would we have been too young to understand it and put it into action?

Well, to my readers, if you have got this far, I hope you have enjoyed the read. I hope it has stirred up some happy memories for you and given you some thoughts about your own journey through life. From its ups and downs to its busy or quieter times, all of which contribute to the person you are today – the best you can be. Writing this book has been a joy for me, something I would never have thought I could do. Over the several months I have been writing, I have found out a lot about myself, both past and present.

A VERY WORTHWHILE THING TO DO.

THANK YOU so much for reading my autobiography.

Colin Thirde.
Incarnascope.

"Iroquois"
111, Green Lane,
St. Albans, Herts.

January 13th., 1955.

Your Progressive Symbol is The Closed Drawbridge and this
Symbol you will have to work with throughout this Incarnation.
Many doors will be closed to you in this life and this is not
a hindrance to you - but it does mean that you have to put your
very best into evevrything that you do* and to realise that
only the very best is good enough. You must keep control of
your emotions and do not be too sentimental - one of your lessons
is "all that glitters is not gold" by your Symbols you will have
a very interesting and progressive life - and it is a very long
life - a kind of very interesting FIGHTING life and you are
going to win through in this Incarnation.

You are very sensitive - and can feel things very deeply -
but you have that gift of keeping much of this HIDDEN. You
have great strength of character which has been built up
in previous Incarnations and will manifest in this one.
Now I feel with you that life should offer you, and you would
be wise to accept work in the Healing of humanity - the doctor
the nurse - if you take up nursing and you work hard you will
rise to be Matron of a good establishment. It is fighting all
the way - for yourself and for others and you have it in the
center of your being - your keynote is service and you must
give that service sooner or later - queerly enough the symbols
show service in an institution where there are mental patients.
I see very distinctly the NURSE with you - perhaps she is a Symbol
but she represents many branches of hospital work - many doors
to knock upon - some remain shut - but others will open if you
knock long and loud enough. The ability to do this work is in
the centre of your being - if you do not do it in this life and
follow another Path I see you will come again to do the work I see.
Time is infimitisimal - it is measured by man and is always tricky-
but the life of SERVICE must be yours and you must QUEST for it.

Looking backwards I find you living in the Island of Rhodes
with the Knight Templars and you show me very distinctly your
Knight Templar Cross. You were male in this Incarnation and
was a very old soul then - having done healing work in other lives
and in other lands. The paternal member of your family was
a Knight Templar holding rather high office.

Colin Thirde. Continued Page 2.

He was a fighting man and also a builder - he was in charge of
many groups of workers and saw much persecution and much sorrow.
You were a younger child born into this family - very sensitive-
a little bit of odd man out - given to emotional outbursts and
crying for what would outwardly appear to be nothing - but the
soul was very receptive to conditions - because of your diffiuclt
temperament you were sent when you were about 12 years of age to
Malta - your education up to that date had been quite good and you
seem good at speaking several languages which you seem to pick up
by hearing. Here you meet with an elderly man who teaches you the
rudiments of nursing in a hospital - you do all manner of work which
is arduous and demands of you much time - great changes take place
within the centre of your being - for you help to heal and nurse
these Knights who have fought in battle and been badly wounded.
You seem to develope this side of your life extensively after you
are away from your home life - study and grow to manhood with a
lot of knowledge of healing and also a magnetic power which developed
in your work and made you most successful with your patients.
It would seem that you qualified in some way on this level for I
see that late in life you have acquired the Cloak and Maltesee
Cross which seems to be a white stone like Mother of Pearl in a
gold setting. I see you greatly respected among your fellows - I see
you in manhood - Tall slim figure - head erect - shoulders back
with long slender sensitive hands which you used to talk with in a
very gentle way - having made very great progress.
At a later date there was a serious disturbance which brought this
very beautiful life to a close.
There is a distinct link of this past life with the present life.

You show me many Incarnations:- India. India. Tibet. China. China. Wales
Greece. Crete. Egypt. back to Atlantis. England. Scotland. England.
The one I have done for you was a very beautiful life one in which
you made much Spiritual Progress and that is the Keynote of this
work.

You show me the symbol of The Rams' Horn. This has something
to do with the wool trade - you have been a Farmer in England.
this about 200 years ago. Now you show me that you are destined
to be a leader of men - you need to be careful what you are
leading and keep out of politics. You can make mistakes here
serious ones. Domination is not your key - and power must be
tempered with discretion. Fight for Humanity in this life by
healing - you would fail in politics. You cannot do any good
taking from one class of the community - those with money have
earned it in past incarnations and build up their own Karma to
overcome - those who seek to take it from them, does likewise.
Judge not others - go forward in Healing work.

Now may the Most High Bless your Journey through your long and
interesting life - the watchword "ALL MUST BE FOUGHT FOR".

     Yours in service.
     Iris Helan.

Milton Keynes UK
Ingram Content Group UK Ltd.
UKHW020330040424
440540UK00001B/3